THE BROKEN SPIRAL

THE BROKEN SPIRAL
Published in 2017 by Mutiny Publishing

ISBN : 978-1-5272-1582-5

Cover image is an original design created by
PINK KONG Animation studios. For more
information visit www.pinkkongstudios.ie

Cover design by Aoife Doyle and Niamh Herrity.
Typeset by Mariel Deegan.
Printed in Ireland by Sprint Print.

This book has been produced with support from Dublin
UNESCO City of Literature, Bodytonic, Mutiny
Publishing and the Irish Writers Centre.

THE BROKEN SPIRAL

An Anthology of Irish Short Stories
in Aid of the
Dublin Rape Crisis Centre

Edited by R. M. Clarke

CONTENTS

FOREWORD

The spiral, that ancient Celtic motif, is the symbolic expression of the mission of the Dublin Rape Crisis Centre. We aim to prevent the harm and heal the trauma of sexual violence. The spiral, with its concepts of warmth and energy, is a reminder that despite the desperately damaging trauma of sexual violence, people can heal. People do heal.

In 2016, Dublin Rape Crisis Centre had 13,300 contacts to its services, seeking help and support. That support was given to people who had recently suffered rape or other sexual violence – as well as to those who had been victims of such violence months, years or even decades previously. That help was available through the National 24-Hour Helpline (1800 77 88 88) run by the Dublin Rape Crisis Centre, through supporting people as they received medical assistance and gave forensic evidence at the Sexual Assault Treatment Unit, through supporting people who had to give evidence to the Gardaí or the courts and through face-to-face therapy. The aim of the Centre is to ensure that as victims of sexual violence go through their journey, they are supported and helped towards healing.

In addition to our direct services, we trained almost 2,000 professionals in the health, education and justice sectors, so that they could better support other victims of sexual violence that those professionals come across in their work. We also used the experience and expertise that we have, based on our work, in order to contribute to public debate on the topic of sexual violence, and to provide evidence to those in power who make policies and laws that affect victims of these crimes.

Based on the evidence available – and there isn't enough state research on the topic – it is likely that in the course of their lifetime, 42% of women and 28% of men in Ireland have experienced some form of sexual violence in their lifetimes. Most people who are raped or otherwise assaulted will know the person who commits the harmful crime. In many cases, it will be their partner or a member of their family.

We know that the work done by the Centre with the victims of rape or sexual abuse is helpful. We have seen people heal. Our committed staff and volunteers know the help that they give is appreciated. But, we must do more. We need more funds to help those who need services who are on our waiting lists. We also need more discussion, more debate in public forums. We need people to better understand the harm that sexual violence does and to refuse to tolerate it.

This book is important. This initiative by author R.M. Clarke, one of the amazing volunteers at the Centre, bringing together such a powerful group of writers with such important stories, will build our resources for services and will also elevate the level of debate and discussion, allowing people to understand the harm of sexual violence and the hope of healing. All of us at Dublin Rape Crisis Centre are immensely grateful to R.M. Clarke, and to all the writers who have contributed to the anthology for their generosity with their talents and for their commitment to our mission.

Noeline Blackwell
CEO of the Dublin Rape Crisis Centre

INTRODUCTION

How do we decide what to believe? Is it the way words link together in a sentence spoken, how the words are sounded out? Is it the way words are plucked from the great tangled pile of possibility and arranged in the correct order of meaning so as to convince, to cajole, to persuade? What makes some words more believable than others?

The work of the Dublin Rape Crisis Centre is built upon belief. Belief is necessary in an organisation that, since their state funding was cut after Ireland's economic collapse, must go above and beyond to not quite make ends meet. It is necessary when they continuously, tirelessly, lobby for change in government policy, in media and broadcasting guidelines, in social reform, even when their work to change beliefs founded on ignorance and fear is resisted time and again. At the deepest and simplest level, the Dublin Rape Crisis Centre works with belief by offering it to the thousands of people who walk through their doors each year; who use their helpline; who they accompany to court; who they counsel at the Sexual Assault Treatment Unit at the Rotunda Hospital. At the core of everything they do is the phrase that in its simplicity has the power to heal the decisions made at every level of our society against trusting the words of rape and sexual assault survivors: 'I believe you.'

This is an anthology bound by writers who believe in the work of the Dublin Rape Crisis Centre. United by a single theme, 'the long and winding road back', a cohesive collection has come together that is united by what is fundamental to us all: being heard and believed and accepted for all of who we are, wherever we are in our lives. Stripped back to the bones of things, these powerful stories outgrow old names and choose new ones in their place, assigning new meaning to a new identity on the other side of survived trauma. In this way, *The Broken Spiral* is an anthology which seems to emerge from the shadow of a dark dream, from a needling, haunting sense of unease and memories of it that recur again and again, into the pockets of light that point to another way, a way that is not defined by trauma, but instead acknowledges it and grows from it, forging a route out of the labyrinth.

The broken spiral, the symbol of the Dublin Rape Crisis Centre, is emblematic of the winding, re-winding, and often circuitous journey towards healing that many survivors of trauma face. But through the redemptive power of the stories in this collection, *The Broken Spiral* anthology aims to bring hope to the reader, and rest; to re-establish a belief that coming out from under the shadow of trauma is possible. What the Dublin Rape Crisis Centre does when it offers belief to so many who come to their doors in search of it, is to give – when it seems impossible, or even terrifying – the gift of connection, which is another word for love. Over and again through the stories in this anthology, love shows up as the glue that holds everything – shakily, precariously, threatening to collapse – together. Love is the flint of light that leads the way out.

Whether it is on a local Dublin radio station, or on the most looked upon podium of the world stage, some who possess the biggest public platforms continue to spout untruths, so far from love, that have underpinned social beliefs and legislation for too long. In Ireland, as abroad, we still persist for our rights to bodily autonomy and to be heard, to be believed, when we repeat, quietly, our voices bowing at the edges, that we did not ask for this. This is a collection in aid of the Dublin Rape Crisis Centre, but the work that this organisation does extends far beyond what is so often perceived as 'just' a woman's issue. It is about injustice at a fundamental level regardless of gender, class, or race; or any of the categories used to divide us. It is about how to tip the balance back towards equality, so we are heard loud and clear, and believed, without qualification.

It seems impossible to believe that this is a conversation that still must be had, that these are truths that must still be enunciated, loudly and clearly and persistently. It is a conversation that so many of us are tired of, but we will continue to have it for as long as is necessary.

R. M. Clarke
Dublin, October 2017

ROISÍN O'DONNELL

Roisín O'Donnell's debut short story collection, *Wild Quiet*, was published in 2016 by New Island Books; it was listed as one of *The Irish Times'* Favourite Books of 2016 and was shortlisted for the Kate O'Brien Award and the International Rubery Book Award, and longlisted for the Edge Hill Short Story Prize. Her stories have been published in *The Stinging Fly*, *The Irish Times* and elsewhere, and feature in *Young Irelanders* and in the award-winning anthologies of Irish women's writing *The Long Gaze Back* and *The Glass Shore*. Nominated for a Pushcart Prize and the Forward Prize, Roisín's work has been shortlisted for many international awards, including the Hennessy New Irish Writing Award. In 2015, Roisín was awarded a Literature Bursary from the Arts Council of Ireland. She lives in Dublin.

How to Build a Space Rocket

You will need:
- Matches with red tips
- A paper clip (colour doesn't matter but red ones would be better)
- The tin-foil from 5 days of sandwiches
- Some scissors

Step 1: Understand what your rocket needs to do
If you want to build a space rocket, you're going to need some matches. You could sneak them from beside the cake at Ishayu's *Annaprashana* when the mums and dads aren't looking. Your mummy and Seán's mam are standing next to the cake with their arms folded, and if you stand very close and very still, they won't notice you're there.

Wind scatters pale pink snow from the tree by the fence. It blows your fringe over your glasses and flattens your shorts against your legs. Mummy's gold sari billows and catches on the sleeve of Seán's mam's Dublin jersey. 'Desperate,' Seán's mam is saying, 'about that child killed on that trampoline.'

The two mums frown at your trampoline, which has been folded with its sharp metal legs wrapped in Tesco shopping bags. Sanjeev and Seán and the Polish girl from down the street are circling the trampoline, their eyes sad. Seán's little sister Molly is bawling and snotty in her dad's arms. 'But – I – want…but – I – want…'

Mummy strikes the first match. 'You know, Bimal wanted to leave it up. The trampoline. After what we'd seen on RTÉ last night. I felt sick.'

'Shocking.' Seán's mam lights a match. 'Men just don't appreciate danger.'

The two mums' fingers dip between candles, and they flick each dead black match onto the lawn.

'I'm telling you, Martina,' Mummy fixes the pleats of her *pallu* over her shoulder, 'He's driving me insane. Soon as I finish paying for this plot of land in India… Kids! Cake!'

You can grab the matches in the kerfuffle of kids rushing across the garden. Mums and dads smile behind smartphones. 'Cheese! Say cheese! Where's Bimal? Let's get a family snap.'

'I've no idea.' Mummy smiles and grips Ishayu to her chest. With her white-white smile, you know Mummy will look beautiful in the photos. 'I've no notion where he is.' Mummy smiles tightly, and you realise you haven't seen Pappy since the restaurant, when he held Ishayu's head and helped him eat his first spoonful of rice.

'One – two – three!'

All the kids blow and the candles smoke.

'Good job!' The mums and dads clap.

'Here.' Mummy shoves Ishayu at one of the aunties. 'Let's slice this thing.'

Seán's mum laughs, 'Aren't we going to sing?'

'Sing what?' Mummy fixes her *pallu* again. 'It's not his bloody birthday. Let's get this day over with.'

Step 2: Establish mission parameters

If you managed to sneak the matches into your pocket, you'd better quickly hide them somewhere safe.

Run across the daisy-covered lawn, down the side passage and into the house. The bright day has made blue dots dance inside your eyelids. In the kitchen, you're greeted by laughter, music and cooking smells. Aunties are taking foil off steaming bowls of bhuna and chickpea masala. They're unwrapping plates of tuna sandwiches and tipping packets of Tayto crisps into bowls. On paper plates, rows of sardines stare at you with spice-encrusted eyes.

Matches rattle in your pocket. Jangle, jangle, jangle. It's as if your skeleton has come loose. *Knee bone's connected to the hip bone*, you sang at assembly last Halloween, when you were dressed as an astronaut made out of tinfoil. Up the stairs, across the landing and –

'Keshika?' Pappy is praying before Lord Krishna's smiling blue picture. 'What are you rushing around the place for?'

There are white lines threaded through Pappy's black hair. Push up your glasses and clamber between his crossed legs. 'Uff, you're getting heavy,' he says.

'Molly was crying because she couldn't go on the trampoline,' you tell him, 'and Seán and Sanjeev were sad and then we had cake.'

'Is that so?' Pappy says, and then he says, 'Hey… Baba, what's this?'

Pappy's legs have been jabbed by the corner of the matchbox. He pulls it from your pocket. 'Keshika…Don't you know it's dangerous to play with matches?'

'But, Pappy, how does it work?'

He tips open the box and takes out a match. 'See this here? This is red phosphorous. When you strike it like this, it gets changed into white phosphorous. The teeniest bit of that ignites. Then the heat catches on the potassium chlorate and the match bursts into flames. Like this…See?'

'Playing with matches?' Mummy is standing in the doorway, her lips freshly lipsticked to an angry red. 'You really think that's suitable for a seven year old girl, Bimal?' Mummy clasps you by the wrist and hauls you to your feet. 'Outside, Keshika.'

Pappy is still holding the blown-out match that looks like a confused question mark. Mummy switches into Hindi and all you understand is *FIRE, DANGER* and *TRAMPOLINE*.

Step 3: Seek out the experts

Yuri Gagarin was the first human in space. He was a cosmonaut and his space rocket was called the Vostok and it went round the world and back again. The flight lasted one-hundred-and-eight minutes, but Yuri Gagarin didn't land in his spaceship. Instead, he jumped out with his parachute and floated back down to Earth, which took longer but was probably more fun.

Forgetting the matches, you're going to need some other components. When you're at the bank with Mummy and she lets you play on her phone, search on YouTube *how to build a space rocket*. The rocket in the video will say *whooosshhhh* and Mummy will say, 'Keshika. Do you have to watch something so noisy?'

'Mrs Subramani?' The bank man in the purple shirt pronounces Mummy's name carefully. 'Good to see you. Sure come this way. Can I give you a hand with that?'

'It's okay.' Mummy manoeuvres Ishayu's buggy into the tiny room with the big poster of the happy family holding their pink piggy bank. Ishayu isn't crying, but he looks as if he might be seriously thinking about starting.

…aluminium foil and a skewer…

'Keshika! Turn that down.'

'So, Mrs. Subramani, you were wanting to talk about a withdrawal?'

'Yes, I want to make an international transfer from this account to an account in India.'

…cut off the match head as easily as this…

'Let's have a look. Right, I see…and this account is in a different name from your joint account?'

…tape the template to the back of a cereal box…

'Yes. My maiden name. Is that a problem?'

…light as a feather but surprisingly stable in flight…

'No, no, of course not, I just wanted to check…and the Indian account? Is that…?'

'In my name also.'

'I see…let me just bring up the right page…'

...hot enough to burn and leave scorch marks...

Just as the rocket is about to launch, the screen buzzes. A tiny envelope floats onscreen, making the video pause. You bash it with your thumb and a message opens.

'Mummy? What does $s - e - x - y$ spell?'

Mummy laughs and the bank man in the purple shirt also laughs and looks at his paperclips.

'She's learning to spell,' Mummy says, snatching the phone off you. And Ishayu decides this is a pretty good moment to start crying after all. While Mummy is distracted, trying to calm Ishayu down, it's time for you to be brave.

Push your fringe back from your glasses. 'Can I please have one of those, please?'

'What's that, dear?' the man in the purple shirt says. 'A paperclip?'

Step 4: Start creating rocket designs

That night Mummy washes Ishayu's sleepsuits and hangs them on the radiator in the kitchen to dry. The sleepsuits dangle their white legs and steam up the dark window.

'See here, Baba,' Pappy's tired finger guides you back to Question Three. 'How can we make the question?'

Cad is anam _____?

Mummy walks in. 'You're such a control freak, Bimal,' she says. 'Checking my mobile! Who the hell does that?'

'Well, if you're getting messages like that, Latika.' Pappy stands up.

'From colleagues! Funny messages from colleagues in Mumbai! You'd understand that if you *had* a sense of humour.'

'Colleagues, is it? And your colleagues in the HSE send you messages like this?'

When the door bangs and they go out into the hallway, you can take the tinfoil from your lunchbox. This will be an important component of your rocket, so you should hide it under the sofa. Above the mirror, there is a photo of Mummy and Pappy in hot candlelight with dark pink flowers round their necks. Pappy is looking at Mummy without any lines in his hair, and Mummy is giving her white-white smile to the camera.

Step 5: Design the best rocket for the mission
Construction is the most important phase. The best time to do this is when Mummy is on the phone to India ('I'm phoning India,' she shouts at Pappy. 'So could you please keep those two quiet for ten bloody minutes?'). Sitting on the top stair, take out one of your tinfoil meteorites and smooth it against your knee. Then wrap it, without ripping, around the match stick. This is tricky, but putting your tongue out in concentration will help.

While you're busy with rocket construction, listen carefully. You won't understand many of the Hindi words Mummy is saying, but that's okay. Just her voice, happy and excited and lilting and lifting, will be enough. And somewhere across the dark, India is listening.

Step 6: Understand your rocketology

When something burns, it doesn't disappear. It turns into vapour. That's how rockets work. They burn solid material really fast, and the gas shoots out and pushes the rocket in the opposite direction.

Mummy presses her fingers together and looks out at the sea. She likes Bundoran because it reminds her of India. Noise and crowds. Garbage and grease. Candyfloss and slot machines. She's been smiling while you and Pappy have been riding the dodgem cars, and while you eat fish and chips sitting on a bench. Even Ishayu tries a chip, and he screws his face up as if it's the worst thing he's ever tasted. Everyone seems happy on the way back to the car. The grey water carries zig-zag reflections of trees.

And then, on the way home, Mummy tries to jump out of the car while it's still moving.

There's been fighting ever since Bundoran. Fighting that even the patter of the rain, the wheeze of the wipers and the mumble of Sligo-versus-Cavan on the radio cannot disguise. Ishayu's crying has slowed to tearless gasps. You're swallowing the sick taste in your mouth and you're drawing a diagram of a hydroelectric helicopter on the back of your colouring pad. Hindi ricochets around the Fiesta, pinging off seatbelt hooks and door handles, so fast that the words are mashed up and you can't understand any of them. Pappy's hands lift off the steering wheel to make angry swipes through the stuffy air. And then, out of nowhere, there's the road. The road is here. Mummy has flung open her door and the rain comes grating in, and when the N12 is going that fast, it becomes smooth as space. No pebbles or gravel or road markings. Like how if you travel at light speed, you can't see any stars.

Mummy is wrestling to undo her seatbelt, and Pappy tries to grab her but she shrieks and shakes her head so her hair covers her face. And Ishayu hiccups brand new tears, and the vomit you've been holding in your throat comes rocketing out all over your helicopter diagram and purple runners, and Pappy manages to swerve the Fiesta to a stop.

Slam-suck-slam say the car doors.

The shape made by the wipers is a rainbow with no colours. On the embankment, bushes with yellow flowers. On a bridge overhead, a queue of black and white cows.

Pappy gets out of the car and lifts you into the cool of the rain. It's just the two of you, standing with the rain making a mist in your hair, with blown-out dandelion clocks on the embankment and cows walking overhead. Pappy kisses your forehead. 'Keshika, love.'

You know that things are going to be okay when people switch into English.

Step 7: Choose the most sustainable option for your shuttle system

In space, it's very cold and there's no air. That's why astronauts must wear special pressure suits which are very uncomfortable on Earth. A space rocket has three parts which are locked together tightly, so it can't break, even if it's sucked into a black hole.

'Are you listening, Keshika?' Mummy says. 'Your dad and I are taking a break.'

Like small break in school. You imagine Mummy and Pappy chasing each other across a yard with no fences. You want to ask Mummy if this is big break or small break or what kind of break is it?

'Keshika, are you listening? Stop doing that.' Mummy jogs your arm and you exhale, spluttering. 'Jesus, Keshika, are you okay? God, why are you always doing that? Holding your breath like that? You'll hurt yourself, so you will.'

'I'm practising for when I'm an astronaut in space.'

'Right well, very nice, but just…Just be a good girl for me, okay? When we go to India next month…I'm going to need you to be brave.'

Nod your head and think about how hot it is in India. The kind of hot that wets your forehead and trickles down your back. No one there watches Dublin versus Kerry. They don't have Tayto crisps or Club Orange. When you went to Bangalore last summer, after one day you asked your pappy, 'When are we going home please?' And he laughed and said, 'You are home, Baba. This is your home.' And you thought, 'How can home be somewhere you've never even been before?'

Mummy is folding Ishayu's sleepsuits into a suitcase. 'Keshika, run and fetch me your shorts from the bottom drawer.'

From your bedroom window, you can see cubes of houses the colour of cereal boxes turned inside-out. In the garden, Pappy is sitting on the edge of the trampoline, which he has put back together so Mummy can take a photo to post on eBay. Pappy looks as if he hasn't been picked for the soccer team. You tap the window with your pinky finger, but Pappy can't hear you. Blackbirds lift from the rooftop, like broken pieces from a Halloween bonfire.

Step 9: Begin your journey to the launch pad

The most important factor affecting human physical wellbeing in space is weightlessness. Being weightless makes your heart beat slower and causes your organs to get up and move around your body.

Tiptoe downstairs slowly. Lord Ganesh is watching from outside the downstairs toilet. Your slippers whisper secretly across the tiles. The fridge hums and the kitchen smells of Ishayu's drying sleepsuits and tonight's fish fingers and baked beans.

Sneak the box of matches from the drawer beside the sink.

Open the back door slowly.

Outside, it's so dark that you can hear it. You can't see the dew, but you can feel it soaking through your blue *Frozen* slippers, and the stars look very close. Trees make shaggy shadows along the garden fence, and daisies purse their pink lips for the night. The first thing you need to do is find a flat place from which to launch your rocket, but Pappy hasn't mowed the lawn in ages, so it's bumpy with clover and dandelion clocks. In the middle of all this, the trampoline glows flat and perfect.

Seán's mam once said you were bendy as a wee lizard. You can wriggle up onto the trampoline in no time at all. Springs moan beneath your weight, and you can feel the metal legs sliding about on the wet grass. Kneel down in the centre of the trampoline and kick off your slippers. Angle your rocket against the side of the matchbox, like how you saw on YouTube. Strike the match firmly, but be careful not to break it. Touch the end of the burning match to the base of your rocket and then wait.

Ignition makes you jump back.

There's a puff of match smoke. A tiny whizz. And then it's over. A thin ripple of bluish smoke disappears into the night air. Everything is quiet.

Flop back onto the trampoline.

The sky above Golan Mews is grainy orange. You remember when you were on the plane going to India last summer, you saw stars like spilt salt, filling every space of the sky. *We're taking a break*, Mummy said, and suddenly you imagine the grainy sky over Golan Mews is cracking and showing the darkness of space beyond, and you imagine a gleaming space rocket (the biggest and best one ever) pointing into that darkness, ready for take-off.

You are a space rocket.

Get to your feet. Bend your knees, shout 'IGNITION!' and count down 'FIVE...FOUR... THREE...TWO...ONE...BLAST OFF!'

You are a space rocket, jumping,

jumping,

jumping,

flying up towards the stars.

Your feet are the jets.

Your fingers make a nozzle.

'WHOOSH!' you shout as the space shuttle detaches, and the legs of the trampoline squeak and squeal against the grass.

Curtains fly open in Mummy and Pappy's bedroom, making a rectangle of light, like a space shuttle window. First, Mummy's face is in the window, then Pappy's. And in the seconds before they pull the curtains wider and come running, there's a moment when they almost bump into each other. Before all the shouting and the other windows of the house lighting up like a slot machine, for a second, Mummy and Pappy are just standing face-to-face. From the darkness of the garden, you can't hear them over the wheezing of the trampoline springs, but you can see their lips moving, so you can imagine them saying *I love you – I love you – I love you*, over and over.

LISA HARDING

Lisa Harding is an actress, playwright and writer. She completed an M.Phil. in Creative Writing at Trinity College Dublin in 2014. Her short story 'Counting Down' was a winner in the inaugural Doolin Writer's Prize in 2013. Other stories have been published in *The Dublin Review, Bath Short Story Award Anthology* and Headstuff. Plays have been performed at Theatre503, Battersea Arts Centre and The Project Theatre. She has just been awarded an Arts Council bursary for her second novel, *Overspill. Harvesting* is her first novel.

'Nico', an extract from *Harvesting*

I'm wearing the new dress that Mama bought for me the day she went to the village. It's navy blue with polka dots and long sleeves. My hair is tied up in the same ribbon as on the other day when I was presented to my new husband. All the men of the house are there, sitting around the table, drinking tea, talking about the fat clouds, the fact that rain is on its way, and about time too. The rabbits and chickens are dehydrated, they're too scrawny and need to be fattened up, Papa says. Like me. A good soaking will do the ground good and put some moisture back into the fowl. Mama is bustling about. She has baked a cake with flour, sugar, eggs, crushed walnuts and sour cream borrowed from the Petrans. I wonder how Mama is going to pay them back; she must have spent every penny in her secret jar on this new dress for me.

She managed to get me a suitcase which doesn't close properly, so Papa tied the handle with string. My black patent school shoes were polished by Mama this morning with her spit and a cloth. They were given to me by my cousin Olga at the beginning of school last year and pinch my toes badly now. Inside the case there is one other pair of shoes: an old pair of Mama's which are two sizes too big for me, as well as a jumble of trousers and jumpers all either falling off me or too tight. Mama says it might be colder in England, she couldn't be sure, but not to worry because as soon as I get there my new rich husband will buy me lovely clothes.

'How will I change and clean my dressings when I'm there?' I asked Mama in private that morning as she pulled my hair back into a high pony tail, her tongue sticking through her teeth in deep concentration. She told me the bleeding would happen again, every month, until I was with baby.

'You'll just have to be careful not to let your husband see.'

The dog is sitting on my feet, nuzzling her head into my skirt. 'Get that filthy thing out of here,' Papa says, 'We don't want you smelling of dog and we don't want Petre to think you're dirty.' He kicks her and instead of slinking away like she normally does, she bares her teeth and growls. This makes Papa kick her even harder.

'STOP Papa, STOP, she's old.'

'A useless old bitch then,' Papa says, and Victor and Sergiu laugh.

I take the dog gently by the rope around her neck and lead her into the yard, tickling her behind her ears, as she lies and offers me her belly. I sense the man coming towards the house, see his boots advancing, and I straighten up trying to arrange my face into a smile. I rub my hands against my skirt. The dog snarls and bares her teeth again. Papa comes out, ties her tightly to the skinny tree trunk and nods a welcome to the man. The thin twine is pulling on her soft neck and she starts to whimper. I go to loosen the bind when Papa tells me to go inside and wash my hands. The impulse to resist the men is huge, but then I look at the dog straining and see spots of sore erupt on her skinny neck. 'Ssshhhh,' I call out to her, 'Ssshhhh,' as I go into the house, abandoning her to her struggle.

My three brothers all stand when the man enters and they offer him their hands, Luca shaking limply this time, his chest puffed. The other two are making a big show of being friendly, talking weather and crops, and asking him if he had a pleasant journey. 'What's England like anyway?' asks Luca. 'England? Who said anything about England?' The man laughs, Sergiu and Victor joining in. The pressure inside my chest eases a little and I breathe out for what feels like the first time in days. Maybe we would be staying in our country after all, maybe we would be near to Mama and to Maria and to Luca and the dog and I could come visit them. 'Which village are you headed to then?' Luca speaks up again. 'Now don't be rude, son,' Papa says. How is it rude to ask where your only sister is going to?

Papa and Petre look at each other and nod. They go outside and we strain to hear what they're saying. Through the kitchen window we see the man taking a roll of notes out of his pocket and counting it in front of Papa, who takes the offering palm to palm, plumping the man's hand in a vigorous handshake.

'Why is that man giving Papa money?' Luca's voice is hoarse. Mama looks like she might have one of her strange fits again, when Sergiu speaks up, 'Don't act like you don't know, Fuckwit.' There is no sound except for the two men's mumbles outside and the dog's whimpers. She has not yet learned that it's better not to struggle.

The lid closes down, everything falls dark and I crash to the bottom of the well. When I hit the ground I curl up on my side. The air is liquid and I drink it in, drowning. My eyes are shocked open, and I sit up, fending Papa off with my hands as he throws water on my face. Luca is trying to pull him away from me. Where is Mama? I see her through a blurry lens, slumped on a chair staring at the man with a look that is full of poisonous arrows. The man says, 'Is she sick? I will not take her if she is sick.' Mama jumps off the chair and goes to pummel Papa on his shoulders. 'Of course the child is sick, why else do you think this man is getting rid of her? His own daughter?'

Papa turns on Mama, grabs her hands and tells her gently to quieten down, staring into her eyes. It's as if she is mesmerised: her shoulders slump forward, her body seems to lose its substance, its fight, its desire to draw breath even, as she stills to an empty silhouette, an outline of the woman of flesh and blood of a moment before. Mama has disappeared, the struggle over. You gave up on me too easy, Mama, you gave up.

The rest of the leave-taking happens as if behind a gauze: woozy and out of focus. I can't remember saying good-bye to any of them, except I see Luca at the door, his emotions swirling and visible to me, almost too big to be contained by his skin. Almost. He let me go without a fight. They all let me go.

A wail follows on the air, which could be the dog, or Mama, or a fairy cap being ripped from its branch too soon.

The suitcase is banging against my ankles, its useless contents bulging against the piece of string that looks like it might snap. The man doesn't slow down, even though his legs are twice as long as mine, and he watches me struggle with the case. 'Where are we going?' My question is answered by silence and a quickening in his stride. I follow, head down, feet tripping in my too-tight shoes, the red dust clinging to the polish and the spit. The man tells me to hurry, that a car is waiting for us and we are going to the airport. My heart is banging so wildly it feels like it might take flight and crash through my ribcage.

The car is at the back entrance to my school and I wonder if Miss Iliescu is inside – can anybody see me with my new husband and my new dress? I stick my chest out like Luca does, before he has to get into the barrel, hoping to simulate whatever feelings he generates to get him through the dark tumbling. It's easier to breathe with my ribs jutting forward, a space inside to draw breath into, and I play that game of holding air inside for ten, then twenty, then thirty, forty seconds. The need to let go is too great and I don't get anywhere near my personal best of sixty-one.

The blinds are pulled down, covering the windows in school so no light can get through, like eyelids sewn shut. I've never seen the tiny concrete building empty before, and it's weird, sad somehow: an abandoned bomb shelter. A familiar smell of sweaty feet and musty chalk leaks through the bunker-like walls and lodges in the back of my throat. Do memories play tricks, tantalising the senses? Already this place is playing out like the past, all of it witnessed as if from a distant point.

The engine of the car is idling and I see a figure in the driving seat. The walls of my heart thicken in an attempt to protect myself from this future – Now. The car is a metallic blue, rusted, with the back left door hanging off its hinges. As we draw nearer, the figure in the front reveals itself to be a woman. Petre sits in beside her, gesturing for me to climb in the back through the half-open door. The seats are plastic, my thighs sticking to them.

The woman half turns her head, her glossy black hair falling over one eye, and introduces herself as Petre's wife. How many wives does one man need? I wonder if we will share the same surname, which I never heard Papa say, or Mama ask. 'Hungry?' she asks, as she turns the key in the ignition, revving the engine, not waiting for an answer. I look at her in the chipped windscreen mirror and see only her painted lips, cherry red and shining. I want to ask where we're going but no sound will form through my cracked lips. I long to lie down at the edge of the well and scoop the cold clear water into my parched mouth. Sometimes, if I feel the longing deep enough I can make it happen. I open my mouth and draw the liquid in, swallowing long deep mouthfuls. The car starts to move and I close my eyes, not wanting to see the familiar slip by.

'Tired?' the woman says.

I nod, not opening my eyes, letting the thrum of the engine vibrate in my body – a new experience, the first time I've been in a car.

When my eyes flicker open they meet the woman's, who is staring at me in the rear-view mirror.

'I'm Magda, by the way.'

I nod, not wanting to say my name. The silence yawns wide and rude, so I force myself to speak: 'Are you from around here?'

'I was, a long time ago. I live in Italy now.'

I try to remember what I know about Italy: it's shaped like a high-heeled boot and is surrounded by the sea and gets very hot in the summers.

'Will I get to see the sea?' I ask.

'If you like.'

'Is it blue or black?'

She looks puzzled. 'The sea is always blue.'

So, Papa.

'Can I continue to go to school?'

'You'll receive an education alright,' the woman called Magda says, and the man laughs.

'I'm one of the best in class.'

'I'm sure you'll be a quick learner,' she says.

'Can I get a puppy?' I say, an image of my dog tethered to her post causing my eyes to flood with tears.

The woman is silent, she looks down, then at her husband and whispers: 'How old is she really? I know what the father told you, but I don't believe it for an instant. She's no more than a child.'

The man replies, 'Good, there'll be more demand for her.'

'That is not our thing.'

I hear them but not really, my own head whooshing with its tumbling thoughts, blocking out what their words could mean.

The car stops on the outskirts of another village, about an hour's drive from my own and two girls are standing by the road-side, two guys about Sergiu's age either side of them, holding their hands. Petre opens the door, gets out, slips the men the same cash handshake he gave Papa. I'm sure these girls don't think they are going to marry Petre. They jump into the back seat beside me, excitement leaking off them, an electric charge in the air. 'Quick,' they say, 'before our papas hear we have gone.' They are older than me by a few years and they seem as if they've known each other a long time. I think of Maria. The shards in my throat tear as I try to swallow. The car drives away and the girls ask why the boys aren't coming. 'Not enough room in the car,' Petre says. 'They'll be joining us later.' The girls look back at the boys' retreating backs. Did they notice the money?

The car builds up speed, its tyres throwing up clouds of dirt against the already grimy windows so all I can see are streaks of trees, electricity poles, flashes of green and silver against the backdrop of a bank of heavy yellow sky. The landscape is flat and dry, parched, like my tongue. The girls giggle and whisper among themselves, ignoring me, pretending I'm not part of their picture.

'You're very quiet, Little One,' Magda says suddenly.

I nod, squeezing back fear.

We pull up outside a bar, with a swinging neon sign outside, like in one of those sawdust and spit places in the cowboy films. The sign creaks in the windless night, as if disturbed by spirits. We don't have a bar like this in our village, but I imagine Sergiu, Victor and Papa would come, if there was one. The five of us go inside and it's dark and dusty, wet stains on the concrete floor and walls. Loud music is pumping into the beer-soaked air, and half-dressed women are dancing around silver sticks stuck into the ground. Some of them are wearing only underwear, and some of them have no tops on. I look away. I've never seen a woman naked before, not even my own body. Mama taught me it's rude to stare, so I look down at my dust-flecked shoes.

Magda asks if we'd like Coca-Cola and chips. I nod. I've never had either, but have seen them on the TV in Maria's house. Everyone in America wears lots of make-up and very little clothes and drinks cola and eats chips. I feel like I'm on the flickering screen, caught in the TV box. My eyes can't focus properly in the gloom and anyway they're not sure what they're seeing, like the game of Trickery the boys used to play when I was little, blindfolding me and making me stick my finger into disgusting things, and then eat them. The other girls have gone very quiet.

'Would you like to do that?' the man asks, gesturing to the women dancing. 'It's better than working in a factory, or cleaning tables, no?'

I rub my eyes, which feel like they're being attacked by stinging flies. I can't dance. I'm the worst dancer in the village. Everyone knows that.

'I can't dance,' I tell him. 'No rhythm.'

The taller girl bursts out laughing, clapping her hands.

The man looks at them both. 'Can you dance?'

The same girl laughs harshly as her friend tells her how happy Ivan would be to see her dance.

'Go on, show us how it's done,' the man says.

Magda takes the laughing girl by the hands and moves her hips in time to the music, twirling her around in circles. 'Very good.' I can see the girl is pleased and she takes her friend's hands and they dance together. Magda starts to take off her blouse and step out of her jeans. 'Copy me,' she says to the girls. They stop. My cheeks are flaming.

The man returns with the black fizzing drinks in long clinking glasses. 'Put your clothes on, plenty of time for that later,' he says to his wife, who puts back on her blouse and sits with us at the table.

'I'll teach you to dance, Little One,' she says to me.

'No thank you,' I say, as politely as I can.

She spits some cola down her silky cream blouse. 'Lovely manners, young lady, but Petre here paid a lot for you and you'll have to work to pay him back. You do understand that, don't you?'

I nod. 'I'm very good at cleaning and sweeping.'

'That's boring,' she says. 'I'll teach you to do other work, where you'll earn much more money and get to look like me.'

The other girls seem happy about this and discuss what colour lipstick they would like to wear and how they would like to style their hair. I wonder what their boyfriends told them they were going to do. I swirl the drink in my hand, the ice clinking against the sides of the glass, tiny bubbles floating upwards. Maybe I should go the toilet and climb out the window, but where would I go? The fizzy syrup is delicious and cool against the sides of my scratchy throat. I start to feel sleepy, and worry I might fall into the well again. Gripping onto the sides of the table I hear Magda say: 'It's ok, girls, it's just time for a nap. You've a long journey ahead of you.'

FIONA O' ROURKE

Fiona O'Rourke is an emerging writer of fiction. In 2017 she was selected for the Arts Council NI & Irish Writers Centre XBorders Project and for the Irish Writers Centre-Cill Rialaig Writer in Residence programme. She was joint winner at the Irish Writers' Centre Greenbean Novel Fair 2016 and earned the M.Phil. (Hons.) in Creative Writing at Trinity College Dublin in 2015. Her short stories have been published in *Fish Anthology*, broadcast for the RTÉ Francis MacManus Competition, and translated for *Troquel Revista Da Letras*. She wants to be a cat.

What You Don't Know

Of course, the dead man turns up again, his scraggly head looming in the rear view, when all Jay wants is silence, not twenty fuckin questions. Sat there, eyelids at half mast, all cat-like and dreamy. Reckons he is Jay's Da and has a scrawny frame, true enough, and a long nose. Seeing him in daylight, Jay would be hard pressed to deny the shared blood but it's too late, twenty-three years too late, the Da is dead, what use is he? Jay clenches his teeth on thoughts that could make him roar and crash the car for pure badness. There's a junction up ahead, so he floors it, and takes a wild left-turn, making the back-end zigzag and the Da wobble in the mirror, his hair fly away, like after a balloon rub.

'It's coffin head,' says the Da, and fills the car with a rusty laugh.

So, the Da can read his mind. Jay says nothing and tries to drop a breezeblock on his scrappy thoughts. They are squelching out the sides like wet cement. Maybe once he knows things about Jay, the Da will fuck away off into the sky or wherever he belongs. Jay's face prickles with the threat of a redner. He looks up at grey clouds skulking above the rooftops. Apt or what.

'Where are you for?' the Da wants to know.

'A funeral.'

'You never went to mine.'

'You never came to see me when you were alive,' says Jay.

'I'm here now, amn't I? Like I said last time, you need anything, I'm here.'

'I don't. I can sort myself out.'

The other night, when dead Da first appeared in the rear view, a dream memory hit Jay at the same time: some faceless Da had already been ferreting about in his sleep, asking him questions. This wasn't a dream. Jay was sat parked below the flat, in darkness apart from his mobile phone glow, flicking through the news about the motorway pile-up. The Da's face in the mirror shone extra-pale. His shoulders were clad in a grey suit jacket, same as now. Yammering away, he was doing Jay's head in with all this *I'm here for you* bollocks, when all Jay wanted was to bite his nails and think about what to do.

Jay slows down for traffic lights.

'You may head on,' he says, watching for the amber. 'I'm too busy to talk.'

'Wouldn't leave you on your own now, son.'

'Never worried you before.'

A car idles alongside his, and Jay catches a female's glance and her barely held-back smile. Jay's cheeks fire up. He lowers his head so his hair can shield the redner.

'You got that from me,' says the Da. 'Uncontrollable face rage.'

'You can have it back.'

'It dies with you. Look at me, Mister Cool, you can say anything, it won't take a fizz.' The Da indicates his milky face. 'Anyway, odd time for a funeral, the afternoon? Who's dead?'

Jay sticks the foot down as the light changes.

'No one you'd know.'

'A friend?'

'A lorry driver.'

'What's he like?'

'Probably like you, dead, only mangled.'

The Da cackles.

'What's he called, son?'

'McBastard.'

'Very good. Have you not got a suit? Them jeans is more for the pub.'

'They're black, aren't they? So's my shirt.'

'You dress that way all the time, so you do.'

Jay tuts. What does he want, for Jay to go, *Oh, have you been watching over me, Father?*

Jay drives past a shopping centre, the outside swarmed with taxis, and men stood about with takeaway cups. It must be shite driving for a living, a face always hogging your mirror, and the *do I/don't I talk to this stranger* malarkey hanging over you all day. Jay tuts at the cut of a bear-sized man in joggy bottoms, like your man ever jogged a day in his life or walked the length of himself. Lazy bastard just wants easy access. Jay closes his eyes for a moment.

'Could you not have wore your wedding suit?' asks the Da.

Fly man, fishing for details.

'No one will be in a suit,' Jay says. 'Lorry drivers don't wear suits.'

'Too bloody fat, son, you're not wrong there.'

Jay starts laughing, then catches himself on. Don't encourage him.

'You're not fat, son,' says the Da. 'You can't fatten a thoroughbred.'

'Proud of me now, are you?'

'Never had a chance,' the Da goes, 'Your ma kicked me out on me ear. And that was that.'

'Join the club,' says Jay. 'She took off to Scotland and forgot to pack me.' He just misses the turn-off he wants, forcing him to go around again, on the roundabout. 'Can you not shut up for a while?'

'You talk to me then,' says the Da, in a shoulder-huggy voice, like a drunk on the tap. 'Tell me about when you were a nipper, say, or a teenager. Did you chase skirt or hit the books? Did you smoke dope or take to the swall?'

Jay eyes the Da, in the mirror. 'I was in a children's home till they turfed me out to a block of flats full of Care in the Community psychos, I went to the College of Knowledge, did some certificates, got a job, moved to a better flat, nothing much to tell.'

'No wife, no kids?

'A girlfriend, no sprogs.'

'Where's the girl today then? Would you not take her out for a spin? Women love funerals.'

'She's at work. She doesn't know.'

'But you done alright, son? You have someone to love and you have a car. I never had the money for a car.'

'Why? Were you pissing it up a wall?' Jay says under his breath.

The Da's face drops stung-like, his eyes settle into miserable but hopeful, like a dog waiting on a stroke or a kick. 'Only wanted to know what you were like as a wee lad,' he says quietly, 'Wouldn't harm you to give a few details.'

Jay looks away. A Merc passes, driven by an old man, with fluffy white hair. Jay heaves in a sigh.

'When I was a wee lad,' he says, 'I thought it was illegal for old people to drive. If I saw one in a car like that fella, I near shit myself…What else? One day I discovered I didn't like cheese, so I threw my cheese sandwich down the toilet, or I would've been shouted at for wasting grub. Then I got shouted at for blocking the bog. The last time I went to Mass, it was the secondary school Mass for first years. The priest said *Body of Christ*, I said, *Amen*, stuck my hand out, and he gave it to the fella next to me, left me stranded, a big beamer on my face, and no communion. I thought it was cuz I was a bad wee bastard and he knew what I was at. I never went back.'

'Ach, you're better off out of Mass,' says the Da. 'Will there be Mass at this funeral?'

'The funeral's finished. I'm heading to the graveyard.'

'Making sure he's really dead?'

In the mirror, the Da's eyebrows are up and waiting, same way Jay's go when he's scanning a room full of strange folk. Jay does look like the Da, right enough. The Da starts smiling, his cheeks deepening the laughter lines around his eyes. Jay feels a stupid smile trying to stretch his bake. Doesn't mean he's gone all family-friendly. Jay breaks their staring match and sees that he's on a dual carriageway. Funny how he's been driving without noticing. How long for, a half hour, a minute, a few seconds? He tries to picture the roads just passed and nothing sticks. He's about another twenty miles to do.

'Yeah, to make sure he's dead, as dead as you, Da.'

The Da just laughs at that, nodding his head in the direction of his window, like he's seen a mate on the grass verge.

'Road kill is not a pretty sight,' he says. 'Decapitated heads and so on in the spectacular cases. You'd be as well slowing down. Hardly want to join the lorry driver, do you?'

Jay lifts his foot a wee bit off the accelerator, presses the button for the window, enough for cool air on his face.

McBastard's dead alright, so said the news. And his ten-year-old son, a passenger in the cab. And five car drivers that the lorry totalled with McBastard's jack-knife. Probably mid blow-job. Jay squeezes his eyes, tries to unthink that, but too late, it's in his head now.

'You can tell me anything,' says the Da.

'Pity you didn't offer when you were alive.'

'I'm trying here, son.'

'Yeah, what you don't know can't harm you,' Jay says.

'I'm dead a few years, nothing can harm me. I died at forty. Don't worry, it's not hereditary.'

Jay shrugs his eyebrows. Dead at forty. Only seventeen years to go.

'Don't think like that,' says the Da.

Jay says nothing and looks in the wing mirror at the chain of passing cars.

The news said McBastard was forty-one. Hard to picture him ten years older. Hard to picture him dead. Good enough for him. Dead like the Da in the back of the car.

Jay's stomach lurches. He glances over his shoulder.

'Can I ask you something?'

'Fire ahead,' says the Da.

'Can all dead people go wherever they like?'

'That, I don't know, I'm only finding my feet.'

Still a useless prick then.

The mirror reflects the sad dog eyes again. Does this mean the Da really knows all that Jay's thinking and pushing away by squeezing his eyes shut? Can the old man flick through everything like seasons on Netflix? Jay breathes in to try and stave off a beamer, but the heat crawls up his neck.

'You had a dream about me, that means you were calling me,' says the Da. 'And that's why I'm here. You want my advice? I wouldn't give him the steam off my piss if I were you.'

'Dunno what you're talking about.'

'Did he start off acting like a stand-in da?' the Da asks.

Jay sends him daggers in the rear view.

''Spose you know all the details already?' he yells. 'Just here to wind me up, is that it?'

'I'm here to help.'

'Is this your fuckin community service or something for being a shite da?'

'It's a promise I made meself – to help you at least once.'

Jay makes a fist to thump the dashboard but that will only make him yell more, say too much. He drops his hand.

Promises. Fuck that shit. Promises want big thank yous in return, that's where they get you. Clenching his teeth extra hard, for a moment Jay feels they could break, cut into his gums, hack his tongue to shreds. Sometimes in dreams he swallows petrol and sets fire to his mouth. In the mirror, the Da nods, like it's a reasonable thing to dream. Jay may as well let the thoughts run rampage, the Da's reading him like a fuckin Kindle.

A gang of estate boys used to gather at the garages behind the children's home. He'd watch them from upstairs, riding bikes back and forth. Of course, he couldn't have a bike: health and safety, some shite like that. If they spotted Jay outside the estate, they would circle him, their bikes at unnatural angles, front wheels in the air like angry horses. One time, when they'd chased him into the lorry park near the boats, this man appeared out of a cab, and jumped to the ground. He stared them all down, a long look at each kid and bike, as if memorising all for a line-up. Said he knew their das from the Ferry Inn, he would have a word, then they'd be in shit street. 'Unless you promise,' he said, 'No more bullying, then your das won't need to beat your shite in. You listening?'

One kid nodded quickly, starting the others off, until they all looked like wind-up puppies about to flip. The lorry driver said, 'Alright, you ever break a promise, you die miserable, now piss off, the lot of you.' They took off. Jay stood watching the man watching the gang on their retreating bikes, going over the small bridge.

'Fuckin wee wankers,' said the lorry driver. 'What are they? Nothing but cunts, what are they, kiddo?'

'Nothing but cunts,' Jay whispered, hoping that was the answer.

The lorry driver man did a wide-eyed glance about the lorry park, like he was checking if anyone had heard, then cracked up laughing, hugging his chest with his arms.

'Okay to curse in front of me, lad, but don't let none of your teachers hear you.'

Jay nodded. 'I've to go now, do my homework.'

'Oh, are you away?'

The man was staring at the ground then, sad-looking like he'd lost something.

'Yeah, I'm s'posed to be back by five.'

The man looked up again, at Jay. 'Aye, well. I'll be back in my ten-wheeler soon enough, eating a fish supper,' he said, nodding at his long white lorry.

McMasters' Carrier was written on the side. 'It's like a wee house. You can have a nosy some time, sit up in the cab, if you want. Plenty of room for homework. But don't tell your mates, I don't mind one fella doing his maths or essays or whatever, but I don't want a crowd.'

Jay nodded and fiddled with the zip on his schoolbag. He eyed the long white truck with the red cab. 'Do you go to Scotland in that?' he asked.

'I go all over,' said the lorry driver. '*McMasters*. What a name, huh? Few of us drivers joke about that, I'm driving for McBastard, it's a hoot, isn't it, kiddo? What's your nickname?'

'Nothing.'

The man slid a mobile out of his jeans pocket.

'Give us your name-name then. I'll stick your number in my phone, let you know when I'm back.'

Next time, he said he'd take him over to Scotland on a run, and on down to England if he liked, and Jay could sleep in the bunk. Jay should keep checking in every month to see what run he was on. Only, every first Tuesday, when Jay went down after school and asked about Scotland, all he got was, wait till Halloween, wait till Easter, wait till summer holidays. In Jay's second year at the big school, the texting stopped and Jay's couple of pathetic little *Where are yous?* stayed undelivered.

Jay catches the Da's eye again. 'I'm on my own promise, Da.'

'Thought that,' says the Da, 'not a great idea but.'

'What would you know?'

'Go see the grave, fair enough, make sure he's dead. But do nothing.'

'Aye, whatever…Can you shut up, I'm trying to think here.'

After the crash news, Jay snuck into the flat like it was early morning, and opened the bedroom door quietly. He knelt at his girlfriend's side of the bed and heard that her breathing was heavy enough. He stroked her hair that lay scattered on the pillow, but didn't want her to waken.

He watched the TV all night. Nothing sank in except for the tail end of one programme he had sat through glassy-eyed. This good-looking bird with pink dreads was on about her mother's boyfriend who had died. She was cry-laughing, her cheeks blotchy red, and she dropped her head while she was talking. *I was only a kid, like thirteen, he messed up my life…I had to say to myself, he is so much older than me, and one day he will be dead, and I will go and mess up his grave.* She gave details about packing her bag with toilet roll and handwipes, and Jay was thinking, *Yeah, she took a dump on your man's grave, holy fuck.* He shivered and bit his nails more. *Closure*, she said, *cleaned me.* She looked right at the camera, her face had calmed to pale, and Jay pointed the remote to freeze her image.

Jay lowers his window more, and presses the button for the passenger side. The grave will be filled by now, firm ground to stand on. He could jump up and down just, kick the earth to fuck. Spit on it. Or be like the pink-haired woman and take a dump. Maybe that would shake the clammy grip from the back of his neck.

'Does she have a name, your girlfriend?' asks the Da.

Jay tuts. 'Thought you could read my mind?'

'I'm only being polite. Alright then, what would Lucy think of your big promise?'

The Da's eyebrows are up again, raised and waiting.

'All I'm saying is do nothing,' says the Da, 'or she will know.'

Jay stops at an oblong of fresh earth in between tidy graves long done up with granite headstones. Two temporary wooden crosses say who is buried in the new plot, *Father* and *Son*. McBastard and his kid. The graveyard is busy enough. Three other people, all in different rows, two sorting out flower pots, one staring at a headstone, her lips moving, but too far away to hear if she's talking out loud. Hardly the right time to drop the kecks and bare his arse. The thought alone makes his face burn.

A man and woman arrive, the man lugging a plant in a box. They walk past, the woman in front, and stop at a grave just up from Jay. Jay has driven all this way, timed it to miss the funeral, and now he has an audience.

He could take a piss on the fucker. It would be quicker for a start. Just wheek the zip open, slash, then wheek it up again. Walk off clean.

But that means lobbing it out. And McBastard down there grinning, like he knew eventually one day he would get to see it.

'I can kick his shite in,' says the Da's voice.

'You still here?' says Jay under his breath.

'Who would you rather have annoying you? A da you never knew or a paedo lorry driver?'

Jay steps closer to the oblong of muck. The earthy smell mixes with a waft of smoke. He hears the woman a few graves up giving off to her man for smoking.

'Can dead men fight?' says Jay, keeping his voice low.

'Not sure. But I'll hit him a dig if you want,' says the Da.

'I don't know what to do,' says Jay.

'Just talk. Get it out of your head, that's the thing. Why d'you think I'm here?'

'You a Samaritan or something?'

'Near enough. Used to be a barman, I got told all sorts. You can't shock me.'

Jay toes the edge of McBastard's grave then wipes his shoe on the grass verge. He turns to leave. The Da's a few steps ahead. He and Jay are the one height. Jay feels a tiredness sink into his bones, like he's done a day's graft with no lunch break, and there's still the long drive home.

Looking down at the bald earth, he realises he is dying for a slash.

'C'mon, son,' says the Da, 'Like I said, he's not worth the steam off your piss.'

'I know you're not real,' Jay murmurs and heads for the exit.

OISÍN FAGAN

Oisín Fagan has been published in *The Stinging Fly*, *New Planet Cabaret* and *Young Irelanders* and his work has featured at the Irish Museum of Modern Art. In 2016, he won the inaugural Penny Dreadful Novella Prize for *The Hierophants*. *Hostages*, his first collection, was published by New Island Books in the same year. He is a recipient of Literature Bursary Award from the Arts Council of Ireland, and is represented by Lucy Luck at C+W Agency.

'Raghnailt's Dream', an extract from *Nobber*

Raghnailt's flicker of dreams have, since the pestilence broke out once more, become so perpetual that she awakens each morning in such exhaustion and emotional disarray that she fears the fatigue and heaviness of these dreams – if their frequency does not lag and their intensity does not disperse – will surely kill her. Ceaselessly her father haunts her, speaking to her with the sounds of lapping water; and she is never certain if he is addressing her, or if he is speaking eternally, somewhere, to himself, and she is only happening upon him whenever weariness seals her eyes shut and sleep makes a grim sepulchre of her brain.

Her father, Balffe, eighteen years ago, after the Boyne flooded and the harvest was ruined, was called down to Dublin to deliver eighty specialised horseshoes to an insane and wealthy chevalier who had somehow found himself in possession of a stallion with three cloven hooves. Gone for two Sundays, on the third he stood in the doorway, blocking its light with his form, holding with both hands a small, foul-smelling item bundled up in cloth, which he lay on the table before calling his family together to see it. They all gathered around as Balffe unwrapped the bundle, exposing an enormous black eye.

It was like shone glass embedded in a perfect circle of grey flesh, seemingly melded together by some master smith, and it was the size of two fists. Disembodied, the eye seemed to stare out at them in calm contemplation, its lower half still bundled among its cloths like a swaddled baby.

'The famine has been averted, and I have become, thankfully, a man with some fat sucking away at his bones,' her father declared. 'Sea monsters, about five hundred of them – though I only hazard, for no lonely creation can count that many at a single go, or remember such large numbers – did catch themselves along the thick mud of that river called the Liffey, and the Dubliners, a skinny people, did have them parcelled into thousands of small pieces within the day. They did swarm in multitudes over the humongous fishes, and each monster was like the length of Nobber, and mountainous as well, but still each was wholly covered by Dubliners even as they were still breathing through holes they employed atop their heads. They moved over them like ants, these Dubliners, because that is how city folk move about their own streets, with such hurry, but also in great and boring uniformity.

'And these Dubliners did cut so many little morsels of the creature so quickly that a mist of blood arose over the whole town, through which none could see the other for the red mist that had blended into the fog. If you put a drop of blood in a greater amount of water, the whole of the water becomes pink, so it is the same with the sky, because over that day the mist did grow lighter until it was pink and the smell of the blood in it only grew stronger, and on this same night there was a fine drizzle upon the city, and I did leave my lodgings to drink good ale as I was lonely without my family about me, and therefore I needed the company of drinking men. I was with a lamp to see about me, and there fell on me many salty liquids and a strange taste was heavy on my tongue. My lamp did grow so dim I went back into my lodgings for fear of going blind, as I was very greatly saturated, even under my eyelids, and once back in my lodgings, I did see that my lamp had been covered in great streakings of blood, as had I been, and that the night-time sky was raining blood. It was as fine a sight as cannot be seen in the dark, but only imagined.

'I knew none of you would believe my tale, and would think I was some loose-tongued scallywag from Kells, therefore the moment I saw so many creatures of such enormity I weaved to the beasts, through this unruly crowd of Dubliners, a breed who are so savage at the sight of food, despite being so listless in the face of work.'

Here, Balffe made many great muscular swishing motions with his hands and his shoulders, showing how he manoeuvred through the crowd.

'It was a great piece of genius to get through them all, but I had my farrier's tools, my tongs and my mallet and the like, and I swung through them,' he cried, 'bruising and breaking lazy Dubliners across my knee like the pups they are, until I found myself about an animal who could have fit me whole in its jaws, and whose tongue would have been a soft bed to me if I were to prostrate myself upon it – and I would venture it was as soft as a woman's tongue that does not tell lies. I perceived, then, if I were to bring you just the meat off its back you would not recognise the proportions of the beast; and the tongue was too big and heavy, so I took its left eye. It was still breathing water out its top like a demon when I did it, and I saw it seeing me, but I took it for my children and grandchildren to have them believe me, because we have never, as a family, been known to test propriety or to strain honesty, and I would not start today, on such a fine, blessed day as this.'

His family, shocked into silence, looked at the eye, afraid to avert their gaze from it, but little Colca, perched on Raghnailt's left knee, had said:

'So it is a monster's eye, and then a monster is a real thing?'

'Yes,' Ballfe said, 'but they do call them whales by the coast and when there are many of them they are called a gam of whales,' her father said. 'Call in the neighbours and distribute the meats.'

The town thereafter packed in for two days to see the eye, and many took whale flesh from her father's cart. Amidst a slew of unruly visitors who crowded in uninvited at all hours, her family perpetually watched the eye on the table for two days, almost making a holy thing of it, until the salted stench of the sea became so strong about the whole town that the priest ordered them to consume its remnants or to bury it.

That same evening Raghnailt boiled the eye, and sliced it into delicate, thin slivers, but her father would only let the men eat the eye; so her two brothers, Colca, and her father enjoyed it. She watched them consume it, jealous, and said:

'I have never eaten the issue of the sea, only the issue of the lake. It does make sense that the eyes in the sea would be proportionate to its size, as I hear it is very large, but Moynagh lake is very small, so it does only have small eyes in it. You know as well as I, Father, that I have always remarked that pinkeens' eyes are too small to look out of, especially as water is very dirty, and cloudier even than cider. If Dublin fish are bigger than Meath fish, are Dublin men also larger than Meath men, and are their eyes proportionate to their largeness?'

Her father folded a slice of eye in half and put it in his mouth.

'Their sense of their selves is very big I will say, but still they are a very small, undernourished people,' he reflected. 'I did see a very big Dubliner, but he told me he was from Antwerp, which he said was not a vicinity of Dublin, but I do not know which province it is in, and he spoke strangely, like a touched, or perhaps heavily retarded, child. On the whole, they are smaller and scruffier than we are, but more violent, though they have fewer Gaels on their frontier, so they have fewer justifications for it.

'But I know your unspoken meanings and you are hinting, daughter, that you are curious to taste this eye, but it would not be proper to bequeath such an eye as this on such a young mother like you. Your melancholic disposition is too great to allow it. The eye might spill out in the milk of your breasts in strange and noxious concoctions once it has sifted its way through your unusually imbalanced humours. You would poison your son with such a sup. You have always been a sad person, Raghnailt, and you know it. You were a sad girl and you are a sadder mother, and this whale, whose eye I plucked out, was the saddest creature I have ever come across. Around me, that day, hundreds of sea monsters were in terror and disarray, which is quite natural, but I, alone, stood before a very accepting creature. I felt it did know me when I saw it, and it wagged its enormous tail in a very despondent fashion. I wish I could show you how it felt but I have no tail with which to express the intense particularity of its emotion, but believe me, I never saw such a desolated beast in all my life, and it would be wrong to pass this melancholia onto you for it might purify those tendencies that have been already too strong within you from birth.'

Balffe's prohibition saved her, for he and his two sons were dead of dysentery within two days, and though they all had terribly flatulent and drawn-out deaths, the knowledge of their own approaching demise was so apparent that it allowed for many poignant moments of reconciliation, and many leisurely exchanges of love to be passed amongst their relatives. Some cousins even came from Kells to make their farewells, and the priest had ample time to deliver unusually luxuriant death rites.

This poignancy was tempered, though, by eight other deaths in Nobber, and her father was blamed for each one. The meat he had generously dispersed had been two weeks old, and the family's good name was entirely blackened.

The only one who had eaten of the monster and remained without complaint was Colca, but even he had been changed by his supper with the eye. Though only a child of five years, he developed strange peculiarities. His face held a perpetually vacant look, except for when he regarded animals, and then he betrayed so much confused emotion in the gazes he trained upon them that the animals would flee before him, no matter how heavily domesticated they had been. He forgot all the language he had previously known up to that point, and began neighing like a colt or singing in birdsong when in distress. The child no longer responded to his mother's calls, or played with other children. Raghnailt recognised intimately the change in her son. He grew selfish and fawning, a nervous dog in his movements. Society did not concern him. For a family as proud and respected as hers had once been, having Colca as its only and last representative was a burden that daily broke her heart. In her mind, he had ingested the properties of an unworldly creation, and in return for his life, he had bartered away his human traits.

She is dreaming of her father again, but, in lieu of his head, atop his neck is the enormous black eye. He sits with Colca on his knee, whose head is also an eye, but Colca's body is that of a grown man's, and he is naked and sprawling, careless in his movements. They are sitting on a chair by an open door, so she knows the world of her dream is set somewhere in the past, for they no longer have any chairs in this house.

'Now,' her father says to her, nodding his eye. 'Now.'

De Fonteroy storms in through the door, pulling at it so hard he both upsets its worn hinges, and awakens her from her light and troubled sleep. He stands where her own father once stood eighteen years ago when he returned from his journey, and for a moment she thinks it is him, but this man before her is formed very differently, in body and spirit, to her father. She grips onto Alannah, who sleeps next to her every night, in fear. Alannah pushes her away, sleepily, turning on her side.

'Now,' de Fonteroy says.

SAM BLAKE

Sam Blake's debut novel, *Little Bones* (Bonnier Twenty7), was an *Irish Times* and *Sunday Times* bestseller, spending eight weeks in the *Irish Times* Top 10, with four weeks in the Number 1 slot. *Little Bones* introduces Garda Detective Cat Connolly – what appears to be a routine break-in has devastating consequences when Cat finds a baby's bones concealed in the hem of a vintage wedding dress. The second book in the Cat Connolly trilogy was released by Bonnier Zaffre in spring 2017. Sam Blake is a pseudonym for Vanessa Fox O'Loughlin, the founder of The Inkwell Group publishing consultancy and the national writing resources website Writing.ie.

The Horse

The stallion flared its nostrils and tossed its head, showing the whites of its eyes, bright in the darkness. Its piebald coat was matted with mud, white crinkled mane so long it had to knock its head back to clear it out of its eyes. Rain stinging his back through his thin hoodie, Jazz O'Connor took a step forward, the frayed nylon rope halter ready in his hand. He shivered, partly with excitement, partly from the wind that whipped across Keane's Field catching plastic carrier bags and abandoned paper coffee cups, tossing them like confetti through the deep puddles slick with oil. The cold bit deep into his skinny frame – he was always cold, he was used to that, but this was a different cold, even the horse felt it, his breath steaming in the night air.

In the distance, Jazz could hear sirens, the screech of wheels as joyriders criss-crossed the estate, dogs barking, snatches of music. The horse could hear it too, and towering over the boy, the stocky cob lifted its head from the grass it had been cropping and gave another snort, poised to turn and run. Jazz could smell him, the horsey scent catching in his throat. In the distance, half-finished office blocks rose like jagged teeth, blacker than the sky, arterial roads peppered with low rise apartments, windows lit like eyes. Jazz wondered if anyone was looking out, watching him.

It had taken him five attempts to get this close, building the stallion's trust each time, bringing sugar lumps nicked from the café, an apple from Tesco's. The horse was half wild, he knew that, had been sure that none of the local hoods had a claim before he went near. He wasn't stupid; lads had been glassed over less. He'd come up now because he reckoned they'd be on their own, and he'd been right – it was too cold for lads to be hanging about, racing their ponies. Now it was just him and the horse and the stars playing hide and seek with the clouds.

His focus entirely on the horse, Jazz made a clicking noise at the back of his throat, and took another step forward. One hand out, he offered the sugar. The stallion eyed him suspiciously, then took one hesitant step towards him. His breath was hot on Jazz's hand, his lips soft and thick. Jazz leaned forward and patted his neck, rubbing his coat hard. The horse nuzzled his jeans looking for more sugar.

Jazz reached into his pocket for another cube, his grin broad.

'Here you go, Krypton.' That's what he called the stallion. Krypton, like kryptonite, more powerful than Superman. The horse snorted again, this time with pleasure, and rubbed his head against Jazz's chest almost knocking him off balance. Jazz rubbed his nose, and in a moment flicked the fraying halter over Krypton's ears. He let the rope hang loose, ready to let it go if he bolted. The stallion shook its head, eyeing him for a moment, unsure.

Another snort.

The horse took a step backwards like he was trying to decide whether to rear or not, but Jazz was ready, unafraid. Reached for more sugar with his free hand. Standing on the tips of his toes he massaged the animal's neck, holding it out. As the horse lowered its head again, he ran his hand along the length of its ear just like the Horse Trust woman had shown him at Dunsink. She'd been nice to him. 'The Teddington technique' she'd called it. Jazz didn't know who the fuck Teddington was, but it worked, calmed the horses – even the sick ones. They'd caught seventy horses, wormed and de-liced them, given them microchips and passports. Some of the lads over there really loved their horses, you could see it in them, the animals nuzzling at their necks as they waited their turn for the vet, and then after, galloping off across the dump, bareback, manes flying. It had been an amazing day. He'd got into shit at school and with his nan, but he'd learned so much, watching them, his eyes pricking at the power, the unity of boy and horse, their bond unbreakable.

And he'd wanted it.

Wanted it more than anything.

Daniella had her friends with their fake tan and highlights, but Jazz was almost fifteen now, he needed more than a mattress on the floor in the box room for his own. He needed a pal, someone who didn't take the piss out of him; someone who didn't think he was thick, who liked him for what he was – like the girl with the blonde hair who had come up asking questions about the horses. She'd been interested, hadn't thought he was stupid. He tried to remember her name. She'd been pretty; posh but pretty.

'You're a fecking skanger O'Connor, he's a mad one. Wait till I tell me ma.' Loftie's words came back to him on the breeze as the horse relaxed, shifting his stance with another snort. They'd been hanging out at the edge of the waste ground, watching the horses when the girl had appeared. Jazz had told her about the stallion, about how he was going to tame him. Loftie had got bored and wandered off, but they'd chatted for ages; about his nan and her flower stall, about their mam dying on them when they were little, about Daniella wanting to be a model all her life and being so desperate to get out of Ballymun. The regeneration project wasn't moving nearly fast enough for her.

A slow smile of triumph crept across Jazz's face as he thought about Loftie.

'Told ya I could do it. The horse whisperer, that's me…' He kept his voice low, steady. He'd come too far to spook Krypton now.

As a gust of wind lifted his mane, Jazz ran his hand along Krypton's neck again, down his shoulder. His coat was rough, gritty. Jazz was going to get a curry brush, was going to give the horse the best brush down he'd ever had. He could nick one but he wanted to keep things straight with Krypton – he'd ask Daniella, she had loads of cash at the moment…She'd only started as a waitress at The Rookery, said it was tips, but she'd bought their gran a coat, and not one from Moore Street – this one had arrived in a Brown Thomas bag. He'd been sure she'd nicked it, but how had she got it in the bag? Sometimes stuff Daniella did just didn't make any sense. His nan said she had a job, that she was happy, and that was all that mattered.

In Jazz's book other things mattered, like horses and his Swiss Army Knife.

He'd been coming here for ages, watching the lads on the waste ground trying to see who owned which horse. Eventually they'd got used to him hanging about, and it hadn't taken him long to work out that no-one owned the stallion. Urban cowboys everyone called them – whatever urban meant; they were all a bit wary of the stallion. He'd thrown some lad last summer, cracked his skull they said. Jazz had hidden his surprise, soon found out that the lad had had a whip, had thrashed the bejaysus out of Krypton before he'd been chucked, and how the stallion had gone back around to trample him, to finish the job.

But now Krypton was letting Jazz stroke him, seemed comfortable with the loose head collar. Jazz smoothed his tangled mane. This was the moment when he got to see if the vet woman at Dunsink had been right, if Krypton really trusted him. And, if she was wrong? Well, he'd worry about that when it happened.

Jazz ran his hand along the horse's shoulder, grasped the base of his mane and in one easy movement he was up on his back. The stallion danced for a moment, skittish, unsure. Jazz felt Krypton's powerful muscles tighten, coiling like a spring, could feel the heat of the horse's body through his jeans. Jazz gathered the halter, holding on tight to Krypton's mane, gripping his flanks hard with his knees. The stallion whinnied and flicked his tail. Jazz let him have his head, focused on staying on. Jazz pressed the heels of his trainers into the horse's flanks. It took a moment for him to respond, like he was thinking about it. And then they were off, hooves pounding the soft ground, wind and rain cutting into Jazz's face like ice, but he couldn't feel it now.

Jazz heard his own laughter trailing behind them like a streamer, felt the horse's mood change, like he was having fun too. Fuck Loftie…fuck Daniella and her job, and…well fuck the world…right now it was about him and the horse. Him and Krypton. Just wait till he showed the girl. Just wait till she saw him.

LOUISE O'NEILL

Louise's first novel, *Only Ever Yours*, was published in 2014 by Quercus. Louise went on to win the *Sunday Independent* Newcomer of the Year at the 2014 Bord Gáis Energy Irish Book Awards; the Children's Books Ireland Eilís Dillon Award for a First Children's Book; and *The Bookseller*'s inaugural YA Book Prize in 2015. The runaway success of her debut, originally published as a novel for Young Adults, meant Quercus issued an adult edition in 2015. Louise's second novel, *Asking For It*, was published in September 2015 to widespread critical acclaim. She has since won the Specsaver's Senior Children's Book of the Year at the 2015 Irish Book Awards, the Literature Prize at *Irish Tatler*'s Women of the Year Awards, and Best Author at *Stellar* magazine's Shine Awards. It was voted Book of the Year at the Irish Book Awards 2015 and has spent 34 weeks in the Irish top 10 bestseller list. She is currently working on her third novel.

An extract from *Asking for It*

'So, yeah…I hope we're cool, because I didn't have anything to do with this, obviously. Right. Well, call me back if you get a chance. OK. Bye.'

I hang up. It's the fifth voice message I've left on Paul O'Brien's phone since I got home from school, pretty much identical to the messages I've left for Dylan and Fitzy and Sean. None of them answered the dozens of texts I sent, and I need to fix this, I need to fix this right now.

The principal's office, the huge window overlooking the primary school and the sea beyond that. Mam and I sitting in the plastic chairs across the worn pinewood table from Mr Griffin, Dad standing behind us, drumming his fingers on the back of Mam's chair. *I don't understand*, Dad said. *I just don't understand this. Why can't they just delete the photos?* Mr Griffin sighed. *That's not really how it works, Mr O'Donovan.*

The Garda station. (Don't think about it. Don't think about it.) The silent car journey home after. I sat in the back, my fingers chubby and short in the window's reflection. The view is beautiful, but it feels wrong now, like *that word* has bled all over the glassy sea, shaping it blood red. My dad glancing at me in the rear-view mirror, looking back at the road whenever I caught him doing it. Mam's body was tense, crouched forward, her knuckles white as she held on to the edges of her knee-length beige skirt, random words and half-finished sentences coming out of her mouth. *I don't...non-consensual...good families...I didn't think Ethan was interested in girls in that way...* She said that at least five times, never using the word 'gay', although it's obvious that's what she's thinking. She often commented on how nicely he dressed, how well he spoke, asking me if he ever had a girlfriend, if he ever played sports, or if it was 'just the art' he liked. She kept muttering under her breath, twisting the fabric between her fingertips, until Dad turned up the radio to drown her out.

We walked up our driveway in single file, Mam smiling at Dymphna O'Callaghan and telling her it was 'a shame the fine weather broke. Still, we can't complain, we were lucky to have it for as long as we did.' Dad opened the front door and went straight to his office. Shut the door. Mam went into the kitchen, closing the door behind her.

And I was left alone.

I hear a knock, then Mam's voice. 'You have a visitor.'

I yank the door open. Maggie? Ali? Maybe even Sean Casey, come to tell me that this is all just a misunderstanding?

Oh.

'Hey.' Conor is still in his school uniform, the top three buttons of his white shirt undone, an angry rash on his neck. He always gets that when he's nervous, a dead giveaway when we told our parents that it wasn't us who cut the hair off his sister's Barbie, or ate the last of the brownies that my mam had made for the old people's home, or made prank phone calls to our neighbours. I walk back to the bed, flinching when I see myself in the mirror. My hair is pulled up into a messy ponytail, my face still raw from crying and blistering sunburn, the baggy UL sweatshirt I stole from Bryan's room not exactly flattering.

'I'm a mess.'

He doesn't say anything, not like before this, when he would tell me I was beautiful. Boys are always telling me I'm beautiful, their eyes roaming around my body hungrily, as if looking for a place to plant a flag. When Conor said it he always looked me in the eye, as if he was saying an oath.

'I wanted to come yesterday,' he says. 'As soon as I saw the Facebook page I wanted to come, but I wasn't sure if you would want me to.'

'You saw the page?'

When we were little, Conor and I would take baths together, and I knew his childish naked body as well as my own. And then we became too big to do that, too grown-up.

(He has seen me naked.)

Neither of us says anything. We both know that everyone has seen that page. I think of all the people I know, and all the people in Ballinatoom, and all their friends on Facebook, and friends of friends of friends, looking at me (pink flesh) (legs spread) and reading

all those comments, and calling me a *slut, bitch, whore.*
I sit on the edge of the bed, tracing my finger over
the pattern of the quilt. He sits next to me.

'Are you OK?'

'What do you think?'

I try to sound calm but my voice quivers, yet
another part of my body to betray me.

'I don't know what to say.'

'It's not that big of a deal.'

'Aren't the guards involved now?'

'How do you know that?' I can feel my breath
becoming shallow. 'Who told you that?' He doesn't
answer. 'Who told you that, Conor?'

'Fitzy rang me.' Conor tugs at his shirt collar to
loosen it even further. 'Sergeant Sutton phoned him
to say that he'd be called in for questioning in a couple
of days.'

'I thought they weren't allowed to do that.'

'Well, you know. He's friends with Dr Fitzpatrick
so...' He bites his lip. 'I hung up on him, Emmie. I
told him that I didn't want to speak to him ever again,
not after what he did to you —'

'Fitzy didn't do anything, not really. He was just
there.'

'For fuck's sake, Emma, I saw the photos. I know
what they did to you.'

And then I know that there is no way that I can
stop all of this. I can't stop this now.

I bend over with the crippling pain of it, aware of
nothing but the sobs hacking up through my chest
and a blistering heat building behind my eyeballs, and

I'm rocking back and forward. A bottomless grief. Black hole. Black space. Falling, falling, falling.

Slowly I come back into my body, into the room, and I can smell vanilla and coconut from my candles, and soap and apple shampoo (I don't use apple shampoo?) and then I remember that Conor is here with me, that he is still by my side, his hand rubbing my lower back, his head bent over mine, his lips against the back of my head, whispering *you're OK, you're OK, you're OK* into my hair.

'I'm sorry.' I sit up straight, turned away from him so that he won't see my ruined face. He keeps stroking the back of my hair, and I am four years old, and my daddy is holding me close, and telling me *I'm his little princess, I'm his little girl*, and that he'll love me forever.

'You're OK,' Conor says again, pulling me closer to him. 'I'm here. I'll take care of you.' I relax into him, burrowing my face in his chest, the worn wool of his school jumper against my skin. I listen to the beat of his heart, steady and slow, as he murmurs *shhh, shhh* against my head. He is so good to me. He has always been so good to me, and he never got anything from me in return. (*We thought we could trust you to be a good girl, Emma. We thought we had raised you better than this.*) I see my father's face and I am broken from the way he is looking at me, and I cannot think about it, I cannot bear to think about it. I wriggle my right hand behind Conor, nestling it in the small of his back, the other hand dropping to his knee, making small circles with my fingertips, working my way up to his inner thigh. His body stiffens, and he pulls away from me.

'What's wrong?'

'I'd better go,' he says, staring straight ahead.

I rest my head on his shoulder, swallowing a sob. 'Don't cry, Emmie,' he says, and he wraps his arm around me again. I can feel him relax into it, and I move so that my lips inch closer and closer to his neck. He gives an involuntary moan. I can do this. I know I can do this. I butterfly-kiss my way towards his mouth, ready to give him what he has been waiting for all these years. My fingers move higher on his thigh. He reaches down to grab my wrist, pushing me away, and stands up, turning away to adjust himself.

'Conor' – I reach out for him – 'there's no need to be nervous.' I undo the button of his school trousers. I know that if he's inside me, he can make me forget, he can make me clean. He's so good, he can make me better. He grabs both my hands to stop me.

'No need to be shy.' I tilt my head at his hard-on. 'It's pretty obvious you want this too.' He blushes. 'What?' I say. 'Are you worried about someone walking in? I can lock the door.'

He crouches down to meet me at eye level. 'Emma. You don't have to do this.'

'I know,' I say. 'But I want to. Don't you want to be with me?'

Of course he wants to be with me. He *has* to.

He lays his hands on my shoulders, pushing me away from him gently.

'What the fuck is wrong with you?' I spit the words out.

'I just…' He looks at the ground before reluctantly making eye contact again. 'I don't want you to feel like you have to do this.'

'I don't feel like I 'have' to do this, Conor. I want to do this. I thought this was what you wanted too.'

'I just want…I just want —'

'I just want, I just want,' I mock him, but he doesn't react.

'I just want to help you. I want to protect you, Emma.'

And he brushes a piece of my hair away from my face. I've never seen this look from him before. It's pity. He feels sorry for me. (I can't bear it.)

'Just go,' I say.

'Emma —'

'Just leave me alone for fuck's sake, will you?'

And he does.

And I watch him leave.

SINÉAD GLEESON

Sinéad Gleeson is a writer, editor, and freelance broadcaster. Her published essays have appeared in *Granta, Winter Papers Vol. 2, Gorse, Elsewhere Journal, Autumn: An Anthology for the Changing Seasons* and *Banshee Vol. 1.* One of her poems was included in *Washing Windows? Irish Women Write Poetry*, an anthology of 100 poems by Irish women writers. Her short story 'Counting Bridges' was longlisted for the 2016 Bord Gáis Energy Irish Book Awards.

Sinéad has edited three anthologies of short stories, including *Silver Threads of Hope* (2012), *The Long Gaze Back: An Anthology of Irish Women Writers* (2015) which won the Best Irish-Published Book at the Bord Gáis Energy Irish Book Awards, and *The Glass Shore: Short Stories by Women from the North of Ireland* (2016) which also won Best Irish-Published Book at the BGE Irish Book Awards in 2016. She has just completed a collection of essays which will be published by Picador, and is currently working on a novel.

Counting Bridges

417 post-boxes.
341 hotels (three-star and above).
28 banks.
16 playgrounds.
3 cathedrals.

He works his way through from the highest number (860 – streetlights) to the lowest (1 – river). When the nights are too cold to sleep he opts for alphabetical, flying over the streets in his head.

A
to
Z

(Abbey Theatre to Zoological Gardens).

Sleep is elusive, impossible, but all energy is needed for the days of wandering. Pinballing around the city, waiting to be moved on. The sheer brain-numbing fucksakeness of it. Being kinetic in a city isn't as easy as it sounds. Plugging into that energy from the outside, not being on the grid.

In the mornings, he people-watches. Swarms of corporate types bound for glass-glinted buildings. Purposeful women in trainers; expensive heels swinging from tote bags on suit-jacketed shoulders. At night, he wakes from a barely begun doze at the clack of a heel, the unconfident teeter of a post-club girl pulling a polyester cardigan tighter, hoping in vain for the comfort of wool. He can tell the height and weight of women by the footfall of their shoes without opening his eyes.

Now a helicopter. A dull rotary thud in his head. Something like propellers slicing rhythmically close to his ears.

'C'mon, I tell you about this many times.'

The noise is of bristles, not some avionic mechanical beast. Vadim's banter is usually firm, but not aggressive. It's December and Dublin's weather is two-faced. Some days the sun streaks along the ground, giving the promise of faint heat. On others, his balls are frozen to the path, his bladder swelling like a growth. The industrial brush scrapes past, causing him to shudder. Vadim sweeps methodically, fishing a wallpaper scrapper from his pocket for splats of chewing gum, which he works at with the dedication of a craftsman. A woodturner, maybe. For a moment, he imagines Vadim smiling behind a table at a local fair, circular wooden bowls displayed proudly to passing browsers.

'Please. You have to move now, yes?'

The sleeping bag offers little protection against the piss-stained concrete. Bone tired, he wakes in the same position he lay down in and now a pain winds its way from his lower back to the shells of his knees. Toe wiggle to check. Back, forth, up, down. Moving the ice in his veins.

He thinks of the blue-black tattoo on his foot, the swirl of her name and this brings her voice into his head. It's been a week since he took his boots off, and years since he's been in bed with a woman.

That night out after work was the start of everything. The heartburst of it, the sense that this thing between them was going to take flight. Every morning he'd watch for her coming out of the lift. Over the sea of desks, the right-angled cubicles of commerce. Mock-furrowing his brow at the keyboard. Clearing his throat as if concentrating, his side-eye glances expert and furtive. The light in the building literally changed whenever she walked in.

Was that two years ago, or three?

When spring comes, he washes his feet in the Garden of Remembrance. Up and over the railings, before the park is open and a short paddle to get rid of grime. The cross shaped pool is reassuring even though he is no longer religious.

'Come on. UP. It's not so clean.'
Peeling himself off the ground, he fishes his watch from the damp sleeping bag.
'Do you have a wife, Vadim?'
'No.'

'Partner?'

'No.'

'Girlfriend, or maybe boyfriend?'

'Nope.'

'Ever been in love?'

Vadim leans wearily on the handle of his brush, wondering if this is mockery or genuine curiosity.

'Once. Long time ago. Not here. Russia.' Vadim busies himself again with clockwise cleaning, the question already in the past.

One week it wasn't Vadim, but another man in his place. No words are said and the man sweeps around him. He imagines his body as an outline, chalked like a crime scene corpse.

Her smile flits in front of him now, so he counts car parks named after saints and colleges. The day rears up, a stubborn thing, urging him to move. To enter into the daily pact of crossing streets and traffic islands. To be surefooted on cobbles that rise like boils in the road. He will find Sullivan, who owes him money, but not spend it on a hostel. He cannot bear all that puckered snoring and fatal-smelling feet.

When he spends several nights on an old mattress behind Basin Street flats, a recurring dream infects him. He lies on a blood-coloured couch, the murmur of a party going on around him. In the dream, when he opens his eyes, there is always a small rabbit looking at him. They stare at each other and the creature smiles, before departing in a flash of impressive tail.

He saw her on a July night as daylight undercoated the plum sky. A taxi pulled in on George's Street, and it was her hair he saw first. Longer, but the colour unmistakable. The same rigid swish as when she turned to him in meetings – serious, full of ideas – or later when they'd laugh in the pub. Clothes more expensive now. Taking cabs and not buses to meetings.

If he saw her now, would he speak? Would she?

People have a way of not looking. Maybe she would see him, and simply not know his face. Or perhaps she would, but in the moment of passing on the street, there would be nothing she could say. Too fleeting a moment to stack up all the thoughts and questions.

All day bodies and legs and arms pulse like the river, snaking around him. Stomping feet and car horns and ambulance sirens that now sound American. The sickening engine waft of buses and the passing exhalations of youthful smokers who feel they're too immortal to give up yet.

There is comfort in the green stink of the Liffey, even though he knows many souls who chose to lower themselves into the dark soup of it.

Sometimes, he thinks the ground moves because he stares at it too long. It turns to water, ripples like the river's shadow underneath the arch of each bridge. He imagines her, jumping in now, afloat on the water like Ophelia, garlanded not by flowers but plastic bottles and litter. She is Anna Livia Plurabelle. She is blue/green, her mouth in the mouth of the river. She is a journey to the sea, and he is already far out in the bay. When he criss-crosses the city, day or night, he will look down and see her always. Dividing the city, a dagger of water through its heart, he will never lose sight of her.

East Link.
Samuel Beckett.
Sean O'Casey.
Matt Talbot.
O'Connell.
All great men. All men, except Rosie Hackett.
Ha'penny.
Millennium (he loves this contradiction of old and new names)

There used to be a bridge that shared her name until it was changed and he says it softly, over and over. When he runs out of bridges, when he can't name any more suburbs, when the parks and canal locks and old barracks have all been noted and named, he lies down under skies the colour of a bruise, closing his eyes against all that architecture, all that loss.

JUNE CALDWELL

June Caldwell worked for many years as a freelance journalist and now writes fiction. She has an MA in Creative Writing from Queen's University Belfast. *Room Little Darker*, her acclaimed collection of short stories, was published by New Island Books in May 2017. Her story 'SOMAT' was published in the award-winning anthology *The Long Gaze Back*, and was chosen as a favourite by *The Sunday Times*. Her fiction has been published in *The Stinging Fly*, *The Moth*, *Winter Papers*, and *The Lonely Crowd*. She is a prizewinner of the Moth International Short Story Prize and has been shortlisted for many others, including: the Calvino Prize in Fabulist Fiction, the Colm Tóibín International Short Story Award, the Lorian Hemingway Prize, and the *Sunday Business Post*/Penguin Ireland Short Story Prize.

Droning on

There was Horse Face bent as a fourteen-week foetus on his DFS faux-suede couch chewing his unbeautiful knuckles. 'Fuckety fuck bastard fuck,' he said.

Buster, his newly-acquired geek.com drone, had done the job alright. The flying chainsaw manhacked onto its underbelly after watching a YouTube video posted by a Finnish vlogger with a penchant for metal band Children of Sodom had successfully flat-hatted the Ballymun sky. But instead of landing on his arch enemy Anto's new Hyundai as intended...cut down the washing lines of several women seagull-screaming in the communal garden by the green bins. Serendipity, good timing, shite luck, Lady Karma, call it what you like, the drone crash also caught the attention of fat wanker Garda Mulcahy from Donegal, who hated Dublin, and especially abhorred Ordinary Decent Criminals (ODCs) like him.

'You're not just a fucking eejit or a scumbag or an annoying fucking eejit scumbag, but worse than that, you're a sly annoying thick fucking eejit smelly parasitic woebegone fat-headed scumbag of the most stupefying kind,' Mulcahy told him outside the Central Criminal Court on a previous occasion when he'd got away with a suspended sentence for intent to supply. All Horse Face had to do that time was agree to a fine that magicked into a *cash donation* for an inner-city charity and off he rambled like a turkey who'd managed to hide till January. His business empire involved a car-wash drug-dealing scam up at a garage forecourt around IKEA. 'Insufficient evidence,' the judge ruled. There was no CCTV or other surveillance in the car-wash itself, even if, as Mulcahy tried to prove with unwarranted iPhone coverage…track-suited young men were diving through the giant whirling soapy brushes at 4pm every day, when there were no 'vehicles' in sight. Strolling out the other end 'laughing like hyenas, pissing wet', as quoted by the *Sunday World*. The smartarse reporter interviewed Mulcahy using an unflattering hypertension-flecked photo with the caption: *Traffic Cop All Washed Out.* There could be no room in the justice system for 'supposition', Mulcahy was told by that little pox ballerina of a pansy judge who looked no stranger to an S&M dungeon beneath the River Liffey of a Thursday night. And so it was that Horse Face was to remain semi-liberated. Free for now to head off from court. He went straight on the rip up the Phoenix Park with fellow blockheads, before being fitted with the stay-at-home electronic ankle tag he'd expect to only see in a labour ward.

Back at the gaff, when he began researching the drones, he chewed over his own fate now that Anto was back home (on the run from men who were infinitely worse than he could ever get to be). He'd had a brainwave after reading about a drone crashing on an alligator's head, somewhere in Bolivia, piled up with three kilos of methamphetamine intended for some out-of-the-way village. It wasn't long before Irish crimbos were onto the same. A quadcopter mounted with a Go-Pro camera flew into the exercise yard in Mountjoy Prison. Loaded with drugs, it was intercepted by wardens when they saw a group of inmates rush towards it shouting, 'Gerroumeway, I'm first dibs, the bleeding stash is mine'. Horse Face could extend his business plan to other canny uses. Hiring them out to gangs who wanted to hit rival gangs. Cops in the UK had already launched flying saucer CCTVs to carry out low-risk reconnaissance around homes scoped out by burglars. Irish cops would never think of stuff like that. Neither would they have the resources; they could barely police St. Patrick's Day or the clean-up after car crashes. It also meant he could deal with Anto without having to face him off. He was afraid of killing him still. Mulcahy was bound to have put a scabby two and two together, figuring out the drone crash in Ballymun was something to do with Horse Face sitting around on his arse with fuck all else to do.

In the early Eighties Anto was his proper bestie. A fellow WHAM-haired whippet on a nicked mountain bike path-humping the dank underpass at the shopping centre grabbing purses and pinching Sarsaparilla arses. When they hit the 15 riding birds and drinking more than four pints without puking mark, both were singled out to run errands for the whatchamacallits.

The bomb-making money-laundering poker-playing dangerous cunts who swore allegiance to the highest planks of The Movement and all they stood for and contemptuously built in garden sheds for the love of Ireland and all its ferocious young men who were being kicked in the bollox by their drunk das after a twelve-hour stint in Paddy Power. No, they didn't give a fuck. If importing heroin meant more money for blowing the balls out of London, so be it. 'You'll be doing this for us later, spotty chin, d'ye hear? Go over there and hand this envelope to Mickey-O in The Towers pub and don't let anyone see ye doing it…we need ye to mosey out the airport later, pick up a package, can you do that, can ye, can ye? It's not every little shithead we'd trust, so listen up or ye'll get a slap'.

When he reefed Buster out of the battered Amazon packaging Martha asked him was it the Dyson V6 she'd been asking him to buy for two years. 'No, love, no, it's something much more productive.' In truth it looked like a shite Frisbee with a load of Phillips electric razors glued on…smelling dodgy as a Pizza Hut salad counter, bits falling off like scabby sunburn. Days, hours, minutes, mouth-dribbling dark lone moments out in the back garden staring up at the blobs of glistening light he assumed were planes ready to skid mark the runways at Dublin Airport. It wasn't an easy contraption to fly. It wasn't an easy thing to get your tits around. All the time focussed on the seething skinhead bake of Anto laughing his bollox off out the back window of the Yellow

Ford Escort that carted him and Claire off into the expanse of a Marbella villa future, away from the lost field they'd dumped him in out by the garden centre in Ratoath deep into night, the very last time he saw him, around 1987. 'You're not up to it, stick with selling hash in your poxy ice cream van,' Anto told him. Claire pissing her fucking knickers. 'De face on him! Look at Horse Face, ah stop, this is too much, look at him, we can't leave him, ah don't Anto, the poor prick!' Oh yeah, went on to great things alright. Security van robberies. Arms dealing, the white powder trail in Mexico. Claire shot in her glamorous head by a yellow monkey of a mountain man, stupid cow, though he'd loved her first, true. He got plenty of pleasure now thinking about the worms who got to ride her eye sockets. The first time I saw your face. Oh yeah baby.

Those early days incarcerated at home on Albert College Drive were something of a blunder-wonder. Watching Martha mooch around the house with a navy pliable washing basket, pocked with square holes that she'd stick her fingers through in all kinds of cosmic filthy spider patterns. Elegantly slicing tomatoes for her lunch. Scrubbing toilets with the most lemony Cillit Bang he never knew existed in the EuroShop. Of course they weren't talking since his latest balls-up, but that made her all the more steamingly sexy. He began to notice what she was wearing; skin-tight black leggings plastered with tiny white horses – God bless Penneys – how they made him want to mount her: 'Giddy the fuck up, Martha, my gorgeous green-eyed slapper.' When she bent over like a Russian gymnast to clear out the ashes in the fireplace, he'd no choice but to boot out to the block shed down the end of the garden to crack one off, which in turn would set his ankle-cop beeping like an industrial alarm clock. 'Do me a favour,' she said. 'Stay away from me, ye fucking drip.' He was hurt, no denying. All very well when the drug money from the ice-cream van was dripping in during the blazing boom years. Black high-gloss kitchen costing €18K that she wanted changed to an 'aubergine' high-gloss kitchen ten months later. When the fuck did Ireland get so well acquainted with aubergines?

He rolled himself off the couch when Mulcahy pinged the doorbell. He was primed and prepared. Yeah. Nice day. Just passing. Yeah. Could he come in? Well, no, not really. What for? Nothing formal. Well then here's fine then, isn't it, yeah? He really should take some aspirin to get rid of that fermenting baboon arse complexion or he'll end up on a two-foot wide steel pus-stained trolley in the Mater Hospital squirming for attention and it won't matter diddly shit how many Garda Union meetings he attended on time, with the requisite amount of expenses receipts. He'll have the same zero rights as a mid-stroke granny about to lick the Lord's flimsy thong. His own ma thought thongs were hilarious. She called them 'cheese slices' and said young ones were pure mad for wearing them.

'Would you by any chance know of anyone around here who might've been so unfailingly fucking stupid as to tie a Woodies traceable miniature chainsaw to one of those flying toys from the Gadget Shop, sending it buzzing across the road up there to ransack and harass and destroy the personal property of law-abiding people minding their own fucking business on a Tuesday afternoon?' Mulcahy said, moving up nearer to him now, as you'd expect a cat to do when they lick the pink rubber nose of another cat. 'That sounds mad alright, there's a lot of little bolloxes around here at night time, next door in the park mainly, getting up to all sorts of crap.' Ah no, Mulcahy went on to explain, this wasn't that kind of a toy, but a potentially treacherous one, especially if it landed right on top of someone, and sure wouldn't it be just the bad luck of the thick fucking gobshite; if it landed on a poor decrepit geriatric strolling out of the credit union after securing a loan to get her back garden cobble-locked.

Mulcahy shuffled about with the unease of a Donegal landowner being told to 'fuck off' by the thick famine peasants he assumed absolute power over. His type weren't able for progress. Those big TV-headed culchies with bacon-coloured rage spattered all over them. He wouldn't survive the colony on Mars. His weak bestial bladder exploding with the propulsion of getting there, causing a big dirty splodge some strong fella would be ordered to mop up. When End Day arrives, Mulcahy and his clan would be better off in a snooker hall somewhere, basting their brains in cheap bourbon, listening to Daniel O'Donnell's 'Here I am Lord'.

'D'ye mean dem drones?' Horse Face asked. 'Those unregulated flying pieces of shit that Ireland has no laws to control, not even under the jurisdiction of the Aviation Authority or the Guards or the Army, sure they're lethal alright. Ye can do all kinds of unsavoury things with those.' Is that right, Mulcahy said, is that so. Horse Face called out to Martha to bring him some E45 cream for his ankle. The tag was starting to infect the sensitive skin above his shinbone, rubbing off his Nike Lunar 3's. 'Jesus yeah, you'd want to nip those fucking things in the bud alright,' Horse Face assured him. 'Sure there's info online showing you how to attach a homemade multirotor with a semiautomatic handgun latched onto it, piece of piss, so the drone fires four times...the recoil from each shot pushing it backwards in the air. "Octocopters" they're calling them mad yokes. Multiple robotic bastard hands holding multiple weapons. Imagine the damage they could cause, huh!? But c'mere an' I tell ye, they're fucking pussies compared to the quadcopters you can attach a proper bullet-farting machine gun to. You can fly them to an exact address using a Garmin SatNav with the voice of Darth Vader, straight into an anniversary garden party. Fuck! Imagine it was the last thing your wife heard: fucking Darth Vader giving it socks before everyone's blasted to scotch egg lumps: *Give yourself to the Dark Side. It is the only way you can save your friends.* Listen,' Horse Face added, 'if

I can be of any help at all, feel free to call back again soon, yeah? I'm here all the time as you know.'

It was the summer of 1984 and him and Anto had earned a fair few quid doing messages for the boys and some of the sexier young ones from the flats were starting to hone in on them. 'We better get dickied up,' Anto said, 'if we're going to take them to a proper nightclub like Flamingos with the plates of chicken curry.' He ordered Horse Face off into the Ilac Centre to buy two suits; a silver one for him and a black seersucker jobbie with gold specks for himself. There was a big march in Dublin later that day in protest over the arrival of the American President... if they 'mingled, mingled, mingled' like Top Cat ordered his light-fingered felines to do, there'd be lots of rich pickings in the crowds roaring against Ronnie Reagan along O'Connell Street. Plenty of wide-open bags to dip into, dumping them in the Liffey as the demo banked off in the direction of the Dáil.

'We've got spondoolies of our own,' Horse Head said, but Anto told him he had to learn to innovate, to think beyond the slim constraints of the current slop of King Cocks. The guards were too busy flanking the protest to be bothered with the likes of them. No CCTV or slick surveillance to clock you on your travels; even the Dublin phone system couldn't cope and crashed after callers bombarded a pirate radio station offering prize money for stupid questions. The city was open as Monto legs on army pay day. 'If you take on Claire,'

Anto said, 'I fancy me chances with Titty Anne.' So that's what they did, in a careless whisper.

Martha was away at her Yummy Mummy Pilates Class when the replacement drone arrived, this time a more updated model costing €650, in the shape of a seagull. Skygull was capable of flying longer distances and came with a handy built-in engine silencer. A 'homing pigeon' device on the tit meant that after the next fool-proof assault, it'd come straight back to base and Mulcahy wouldn't be able to pin anything on him. He made himself a ham and coleslaw sandwich, trying to think up ways to get Anto well and truly in the nebs where it'd hurt. It was probably just as well his inaugural military offensive had failed, wrecking his car didn't seem like enough of a payback. He'd been back four months now, knew rightly where he lived, but still didn't think of calling around to apologise. Horse Face would've been made up with a proper apology and a 12-pack of Dutch Gold, the two of them sitting out in the garden reliving golden nuggets of old-fangled days. He could attach a balloon with rat poison to kill off his precious Dobermans, or lace it with blades, hovering at his front door until he sauntered out to head to the pool hall, taken by surprise. He could even fly the fucking thing up at their bedroom window after midnight, using the heat censor to track his wife's jiminy bits when she took her knickers. Filming the two of them humping like crane flies, putting it up on Facebook before they'd a chance to open the cornflakes the next morning.

Out in the garden, where it'd been raining, he saw a big fat seagull stamping its pox-ridden feet to trick a few worms to the surface. He turned Skygull on and let it walk around for a bit until it got stuck in a wet patch of soil where Martha had tried (and failed) to plant roses the year before. It started doing a padding motion on the grass. The other seagull wandered over, wary, taking a quick peck at Skygull's neck, widening out its wings to full diameter, flapping, making a 'keow ha-ha-ha-ha' sound, then again, 'keow ha-ha-ha-ha' 'keow ha-ha-ha-ha' 'keow ha-ha-ha-ha'. The next door neighbour, O'Brien, a right nosey bastard, stuck his head over the wooden fence. 'What you got there?' he asked Horse Face. 'Doesn't look like a normal seagull.' The drone had a dark cap on its head, covering the SatNav and motion sensors. 'It's a grey-hooded gull, a rare species only found in North America, I got it from a geezer in the pet shop in Parnell Street.' He could see O'Brien squinting his eyes, not sure whether to believe him. 'Do you have a license for it?' he asked. O'Brien was well in with that BirdWatch Ireland lot. 'It's only out on loan, I'll be giving it back in a fortnight,' he said, pleased that he was able to scupper him without much thought. 'He likes a bit of streaky bacon but if you're heading out the shops any time soon, feel free to pick us up a bit of dog food for the mite to keep him going.'

Martha came through the door then, all sweaty and sexy, her leggings stuck tight to her muscly thighs. 'I met Anto up at the shops,' she said. 'He's doing well for himself, working as a drugs counsellor up at The Project.' It wasn't what he expected to hear. If anything Horse Face assumed Anto would be back peddling as soon as things died down, not turning youngfellas and youngones off buying the stuff. 'Did he ask about me?' Horse Face said, trying not to think of the night they dumped him in the field in Rathoath. How it took him eight hours to limp home, no cars stopping to risk giving him a lift cos he looked like a right knackbag. 'He was made up to hear you were off the stuff and turning over a new leaf,' she said. 'He's been wanting to pop around and see ye but hearing you were up in court he thought it best to leave you to it, but I put him wide.' She looked all pleased with herself, as if she'd managed to renovate him, turning him into something high-gloss and pleasing to the touch. 'He said he'll be around in the morning, I gave him your mobile number. Put some fucking socks on that yoke when he's here,' she said, pointing to the tag on his ankle. 'I'm bleeding scarlet just looking at it.' They strolled off into the kitchen. Martha said she was going to make a 'one pot pasta' dish she'd seen on YouTube. 'You just lob it all in and it tastes proper gorgeous,' she said. 'All the garlic soaks into the spaghetti, making a right dance in the gob and you put natural yoghurt on top at the end to make a creamy sauce that's low-fat.' Lately she'd got carried away making all this healthy vegetarian slop. Said it was 'better' for him and on account of him having no work, he could look forward to a bit of meat on Sundays only.

The doorbell rang and it was O'Brien with one of his BirdWatch cronies. 'Is it alright if we take a closer look at the gull?' he asked. Horse Face had to think quick on his feet. 'Yez can have a goo through the kitchen window there, but don't go out on account of them doing their mating dance yoke.' He explained to the BirdWatch plonker that they were 'two lezzers' and that the white headed one probably didn't realise the gray-headed gull wasn't a bloke. 'Fascinating,' O'Brien's mate said. 'I've heard of this malarkey before but it's definitely rare. In fact it's unclear exactly why the gulls take part in this behaviour, possibly to do with the high female to male ratio on the islands where they originate. Would you mind if we brought the team here tomorrow to take notes?' Horse Face said that'd be fine, but he'd have to charge them a fiver each to cover the cost of food pellets and 'fancy bedding' he'd ordered off the internet. He told them to call around at eleven or so, no later than midday. He closed the door with a bang and took Martha upstairs for a good seeing to, shouting at the top of his lungs, 'Keow ha-ha-ha-ha' 'Keow ha-ha-ha-ha'.

Horse Face heard them before he had time to wake and see them. Loud chatter about EU flagship nature laws, Birds and Habitats Directives, Jean-Claude Juncker and something something something. 'They're fucking early!' he shouted at Martha. Still asleep in her 'no need to remove at night-time' Bare Minerals make-up that cost a fair few quid just so she could be a dirty bint and not wash herself. He leapt down the stairs two steps at a time, a long queue of nerds and buzzard heads in the front garden with O'Brien as Pied Piper snaking out the gate and down the road. At least half of them looked birdlike, skinny legs and salt and pepper hair of Curlews. His heart dropped like a slippy anchovy from a Lidl tin when he spotted Anto with them. He freed himself from the nerds and made his way to the front door. 'Bud,' he said. 'So nice to see you bud.' He looked older, more rubbery. 'Come in,' Horse Face said, doing his best to contain his decade-old anger. He gave him the low-down in the kitchen. 'You throw these pellets out at the birds when I take that lot out to do their business,' he instructed. 'You're a gas man,' Anto said, 'always up for the scam.' It was Anto who'd been King of the Scams in the eighties, bossing him about like a prize gimp. When Horse Face turkey-chested back out to the front door, he saw Mulcahy had pulled up in the squad car. 'What's going on here?' he roared, pushing by the BirdWatch lot. 'All above board, sir,' Horse Face assured him. 'They're here to study my fine specimens of rare seagulls.' Mulcahy eyeballed the queue of eejits in the front garden, telling them to put their dosh away. 'Are they fuck,' he said. 'Are you doing deals here?' His bright crimson bacon chops seemed even more fire engine red than usual. He limped out after Horse Face to the garden where Anto was standing like a muppet holding onto the pellets. 'What have you got there?' Mulcahy asked, grabbing one of the pellets, taking a small nibble. 'It's food for the gulls,' Anto told him. The bird watchers were streaming in through the house, armed with notebooks and collapsible cloth stools bald retirees take with them to the seaside. 'Food?!' Mulcahy laughed. 'Do you take me for an even bigger fool than your friend here?' he said. 'This is Class A hashish, scank, wood, marijuana,' pulling out his handcuffs from his arse pocket. 'I'll kill you!' Anto roared at Horse Face, 'you double-crossing shitebag.' This was the best of mornings. Skygull had attracted half a dozen fat seagulls to the grass, all hopping and jumping and pecking, with the bird watchers nearly coming in their pants. With Mulcahy making his first proper arrest of the week Horse Face grabbed the biggest dessert spoon he could find, lobbing a load of leftover yoghurt from Martha's YouTube dinner at his back so it looked like he was being shite-bombed from the air. 'You're not just a fucking eejit or a scumbag or an annoying fucking eejit scumbag,' he yelled. 'But worse than that, you're a sly annoying thick fucking eejit smelly parasitic woebegone fat-headed scumbag of the most stupefying kind.' Mulcahy yanked Anto through the house towards the squad car. Out came the throng of bird chasers, sprinting in their corduroy trousers after Skygull, who was by now, zipping happily through the skies of Ballymun. His exotic grey drone head prodding the clouds in celebration.

ALEX REECE ABBOTT

Writing across genres, forms and hemispheres, Alex's historical novel, *The Helpmeet*, was a 2016 Greenbean Irish Novel Fair winner. Her stories have won the Arvon, Crediton and Northern Crime prizes, and '37 Foolish Things' was a finalist in the 2017 Bath Novella-in-Flash Award. Widely published and anthologised, her work features in the Word Factory's Citizen season and has been selected for *Bonsai: The Big Book of Small Stories* (Canterbury University Press, 2018) the first anthology of New Zealand short-short fiction. Among others, her stories have been shortlisted for the Bridport, Lorian Hemingway, HG Wells, Hummingbird, Tillie Olsen, and *Sunday Business Post/ Penguin* Short Story prizes.

The Call of Blood

Hazel tips her brown paper bag and ten green grenades roll across the kitchen counter.

She holds one and sniffs the smooth leathery skin, offers the fruit to Rose. Her sister brushes her off and takes her knife to the chives. Hazel lines up the egg-shaped fruit in a neat row. 'Amazing, eh? They're calling them pineapple guavas down the market. Rowan spotted them. Cost a bomb, but we're on holiday. I forgot to get the strawberries – so we're having feijoas for dessert.'

Just saying Fee-GEE-OH-ah sounds musical, exotic. Not a lot of people spoke Portuguese when they were growing up in Auckland. Not that they heard, anyway.

The word takes Rose back. Back to the feijoa tree. *Feijoa sellowiana. Acca sellowiana* now. Towards the end of the summer holidays, the evergreen bushes that lined their quarter acre used to be heavy with ripening feijoas. Wasps, drunk on the fermenting flesh, would battle at the foot of the shrubs. As kids, they ate the fruit. Cut them in half with a tea-spoon like boiled eggs, scooped out that almond flesh – if they weren't too sour, or too ripe, when the warm insides had turned to gritty slime. The grown-ups called them *an acquired taste.*

Rose waves her knife at the fruit, a green rain of chives falls on the bench.

'You want these tonight?'

'Uh-huh. Why not?'

Hazel carries on assembling the birthday cake that she's baked for their mother. Vi.

Rose swallows hard and jams the feijoas in a white porcelain bowl. Hazel can remember if it suits her. The sepals flare over the edge like torpedo propellers. Typical thoughtless Hazel, bringing feijoas into her home. Seething, Rose scratches at her cheek where a hot rash is rising.

On the sofa, Vi switches off the television. Rose wonders when her mother's skin became a Pollock canvas, spattered with liver spots, wonders if she'll go the same way.

Rowan groans as her grandmother wraps a spindly arm around her shoulders.

'Too noisy,' splutters Vi, going into a coughing fit. Still wheezing, she reaches down the side of the sofa and pulls a present from her handbag.

Rowan rips off the dinosaur wrapping paper. 'Read me this one, Grandma,' she whoops, swinging off the arm of the sofa and waving her new book.

It strikes Rose that Hazel was around the same age as Rowan. When it happened.

Vi pulls Rowan back on the sofa, and points at the book-cover. 'This story is called *The Royal Fern*.' Her voice is deep, steeped in a lifetime of tar.

'Loyal Vern,' chants Rowan.

'That's right.' Vi opens the book. 'A very old story about a king. He wants to protect his family, but he's frightened and he's in a rush. In his panic, he doesn't know what to do. And *then*...he sees...the fern.'

'Listen to her,' Rose hisses in her sister's ear. 'Reading that to your daughter as if butter wouldn't melt. Never mind *The Royal Fern* — how about *The Royal Fucking Feijoa* — we all know that one, don't we?'

Hazel glares at her. 'It's a silly fable. Drop it.'

'Everything alright?' Vi calls. 'Yell if you need a hand.' She doesn't move from the sofa.

'Stay there, birthday girl,' Hazel answers, in her sing-song everything's alright voice.

Rose grinds her knife against the steel. Such a fake.

Hazel holds out her spatula and offers her a scraping of dark chocolate icing.

Rose shakes her head. 'She obviously doesn't remember either, or she wouldn't be reading that — and *you* wouldn't let her.'

Hazel polishes off the leftover icing. 'Leave me out of it.'

'Or, she doesn't *want* to remember.' Rose lowers her voice. '*You* know the feijoa trees.' Every summer, all that fruit. Soft, green, rotting on the ground. They were only good for chutney, or screening out the neighbors. 'Then, you turned up with feijoas this afternoon – didn't they used to make you gag? Remember?'

Hazel plucks chocolate curls from the grater and drops them into her mouth.

'Remember what started it?' She waves her knife towards the sofa, where Vi is still reading. 'Eating with your mouth open again. You were worse than a truffle pig, snorting and snuffling your way through every meal.'

'Keep your voice down,' says Hazel, washing her hands.

Rose stares at her knife. The trick was not to look while Hazel was eating. And once The Animal had invaded their home and taken up residence, he didn't appreciate Hazel's table manners either. Not looking was not enough.

And, whenever he kicked off, what did their mother do?

Nothing.

She sees The Animal as if it was yesterday. Sees him, fermenting at the end of their kitchen table, like something Hazel had brewed up in her birthday chemistry set. Hears his ranting, punctuated by the bread-knife handle smashing against the red Formica. That weather-vein, bulging and ticking on his left temple. Stormy weather.

'Smelling good, girls,' calls Vi.

Rose eyeballs Hazel. 'Not long now,' she answers.

Their grandmother used to say that you are what you eat. The Animal was what he drank. Hair steel grey of a brewery beer cask by twenty-four. Ten years on he washed up at their door. That pocked gaunt face, puce as the *pinot noir* that used to grow in that vineyard at the end of their street. His predator eyes: cold blue, never blinking.

Hazel turns away. 'Let's get this meal ready. It's been a long day.'

'Some things need to be talked about – and *you* brought her here,' presses Rose.

Hazel licks cream from her thumb, adds more caster sugar to the bowl; gently stirs it. 'My head's already full of work stuff. And, it's her birthday – so don't start.'

'Start what?'

'Don't go to too much trouble, girls,' calls Vi. 'I'm not that hungry.'

'Blood is thicker than water, that's all I'm saying.' Hazel splashes dark vanilla essence into the cream and stirs again.

'And so is mucus, but I still wouldn't waste my spit on her,' says Rose.

'She'll hear you.'

Rose snorts. 'Yeah, I'd forgotten that her hearing loss is almost as selective as her memory.'

Hazel peels another long ribbon of white chocolate and samples it. 'It's ridiculous, getting worked up over old crap. The Animal died years ago. And this could be her last birthday.'

Rose stares at Vi. Her mother's face is set hard under the halogen spots.

She remembers that sticky Saturday, late summer. Pushing Hazel out the front door and getting her down the steps. Her mind skittering, searching for safe distance – Nan's, the neighbours' – even up one of the big trees in the back yard. Too obvious, all places that were already known. Needing more time to think, blood pulsing, sonar in her ears. Taking Hazel to the only place she can think of, where they couldn't be seen from the lounge windows – behind the feijoa bushes.

Move, Haze. Move quick. Stay quiet.

Pressed low to the ground, like soldiers in Vietnam on the grainy six o'clock news. Flexing those dense, overhanging branches, open arms that grew long and low. Holding them back, so they could make it to that small space against the trunk. All the while, the shouting from the kitchen carrying the sound of their names.

'Don't be heavy-handed with the chocolate, Hazel,' calls Vi. 'I like to taste my cake.'

Rowan's belly-laugh fills the room. 'Cake!'

Hazel leans against the counter, watching Rowan with a smile.

But, you were there, right in front of me, burrowing under those branches, thinks Rose. Waiting in that cool feijoa embrace. Fingers crossed so hard they hurt. Waiting, knowing that their sanctuary had one escape route...the same way they came in. All the time. The Animal making his barefoot patrol of the property, shouting and thundering, his warpath leading him nearer and nearer. So close that, even surrounded by so much rotting fruit, she could still smell his vinegar-plonk sweat.

'You remember.' Rose insists.

Hazel gathers up her perfect, white chocolate ribbons with a heavy sigh. 'I don't know what you're talking about.'

Rose hears his curses cutting the humid suburban air, hears him circuiting their house again. One minute he was all calm manipulation, temper-fueled outbursts the next. But always a threat. They were scared under that tree, scared to breathe. Drenched in nervous terror, trying not to giggle. The Animal growling.

Wondering, wondering: could the feijoa bush really keep them safe?

Make them invisible?

Spying through the veil of leaves, she sees him stop out on the front lawn, wavering on one leg. Prays that the neighbors haven't seen him. Prays for wasps: he was allergic. Swearing when it was only prickles that he pulled from his leathery sole. Hoping that he'd missed some – then they could turn as septic as the rest of him. Blood poisoning could be fatal.

The Animal was so preoccupied with those prickles from the lawn, he never looked into the shrub where they were waiting. He moved on, searching for them in the high branches of the pepper tree. Ripping open the latch to the space under the house, where they had their den. Wood splintering, the clatter of the gate hitting the concrete path.

Threats and promises about how sorry they were going to be. Even though she was only ten, Rose saw the twist of his logic in his offer to beat some sense into them.

It seemed like they were in the heart of that feijoa bush forever. Waiting, until long after he'd bored with them. Long after his muttering had faded off into the distance.

The slam of the front door, then quiet. Rose knew that he'd be overtaken by some other rage, soon distracted onto another pointless trail. Or, even better, he'd pass out.

They waited. Waited and listened, until there was nothing, except the scratchy cicada drone-song, and the screeching brakes from the neighbors' kids, chasing each other, skidding and sliding their bikes on the loose metal road. By the time Hazel wanted the toilet, it was dusk. The front door was ajar, so inside they crept. In the lounge, the television was murmuring...and there was The Animal. Flopped across the black vinyl sofa, grunting and snoring. An empty half-gallon flagon lolling on the brown floral carpet, stranded in a wet patch of cheap sauterne. They gave him a wide berth, and used the other door into the kitchen.

The Good Housekeeping Zombie scanned them for clues.

Where've you been? We were calling you.

Just playing, answered Rose, because it was way too late for their mother to start acting the super-parent.

Next thing, the Zombie says *Where?* And Rose's mind is jumbling, not ready. She sees herself calculating: say nothing = unsafe. Answer = make safe unsafe. Say something + not the whole story = trigger a full interrogation.

At last, Hazel started coughing and wheezing. *Distraction.*

Her asthma, a perfect escape again.

Rowan squirms on the sofa. 'Go on, Grandma. Again, again.'

Vi snaps the book closed. 'The end.'

Hazel sieves snowy sugar drifts across the dark chocolate, then spears the perfect icing with scarlet, barbershop-striped candles. 'Only one story, Rowan. Grandma's tired.'

Vi cranes her neck towards them. 'Alright girls?'

'We're nearly finished,' says Rose.

When Hazel commandeers the potato salad, Rose doesn't argue. She jabs at the surface with fat chunks of gherkin for decoration. *Don't they say pick your battles? Don't they say never start a fight in a kitchen?*

The kitchen, that warm, cosy, domestic crossroads. A veritable armory, stocked up with meat cleavers, icepicks – and, plenty more potential weapons. Punch & Judy's rolling pin and a few good sharp knives, that's my arsenal, thinks Rose.

Hazel is right. Blood *is* thicker than water. And a lot harder to clean up.

The Italians said it: the call of blood. There's always at least one relative that you're unable to ignore. She wonders if it was blood that called her to action, called her to rescue her sister that humid afternoon on the other side of the world.

Blood and feijoas.

She looks at Hazel. Fifty per cent of the same DNA, yet so different. Like the way they sampled their memories by time and convenience. Once, she'd been certain that being able to recall it all was a good thing; now she isn't sure. Still, it has to be better than facing Hazel's smug denial over the kitchen counter.

Blood and feijoas.

She's been holding that moment in her unusable memory, picking at it like a spell. And now, the splinter is working its way out. She has to honor what happened to them, even though Hazel swears she's already let it go. But, she won't – can't – believe that Hazel can forget.

Not if she can remember.

After dinner, when Rowan is in bed and Vi is watching a re-run of *Casualty*, the sisters tidy the kitchen.

Hazel leans over to Rose, a conspirator. 'Thanks again for having us to stay at such short notice. Cheers.'

Rose taps her sister's outstretched wine glass. 'No worries.'

They watch Vi dozing on the sofa, head dropped to her chest. Every other shallow breath, she lets out a moan.

'She's had her meds,' says Hazel with a nod. 'Just midnight to do now.'

Rose swigs her lager, filling her mouth with clean, cold bubbles. It's as if Hazel relishes coordinating their mother's complicated array of syrups, patches, pills and potions. Like she's competing for some daughterly badge of honor.

'It's good to get away and relax.' Hazel sips her burgundy with a long appreciative sigh. 'Nice crumble too. I knew those pineapple guavas reminded me of something.'

'Feijoas?' says Rose.

Hazel ignores her. 'They remind me of gin.'

Rose wrinkles her nose. 'A taste I never acquired.'

'I haven't told you my big news.' Hazel leans over. 'I'm escaping. Getting right out of social work, getting away from all those needy families.'

Rose takes another mouthful of lager. 'Do you ever think...of the things...the things only you and I know? How no-one else has those same memories, that same knowledge? They're part of us.'

Hazel sighs. 'Such as?'

'Childhood stuff, memories. The things that wouldn't make sense to anyone else. Only sisters.'

Hazel yawns. 'I'm opening a little tea-shop by the sea, selling all my own baking.' She taps her glass for a refill.

'You won the lottery?'

'I'll find the money somewhere – and people love a bit of nostalgia, don't they? Brandy snaps, treats from the past. Still deciding on a name though.'

Rose pours her wine. 'How about *Old Times* or *Good Old Days?*'

'Fab!' Hazel notes them down in her phone. 'Any more?'

Rose polishes off her lager and muses that her poker face is wasted, yet again.

Hazel insists they choose a plant for Vi's birthday.

Could be the last one, she says. It's an important ritual, something special to do together.

As a family.

Rose drags herself around the garden centre, still suspecting that Hazel has lifted this whole palaver from her social work textbooks.

Family Therapy 101?

'This is a nice climber.' Hazel sniffs at an apricot rose. Her nostrils flare.

Rose studies the product card. '*Happy Days*. Maybe not.'

Hazel scans the rows of English roses. 'But not a plant that's named after either of us.'

'That's a shame. I was going to suggest *Corylus avellana Contorta*,' says Rose.

Hazel frowns.

'Twisted hazel. Very hardy.'

Rose scores a point in the air, but Hazel blanks her.

Rowan yawns and begins kicking the trolley wheels.

'Look Rowan,' says Hazel. 'This is the same as that fern in your story.'

'Well, you're not short of rain in the Pennines,' says Rose, cleaning her sunglasses. 'Europe's largest, most imposing fern. Deciduous though.'

Hazel strokes the feathery fronds. 'Alright, you're the garden designer. Let's get *Osmunda regalis* for her. I think she'll like it – and I love the fairy-tale that goes with it. Every plant has a story, doesn't it? To protect his family, the Saxon god Osmunda does this really amazing —'

'Look. *Phyllostachys nigra.*' Rose points out a stand of black bamboo rustling in the breeze. She selects a plant with an even spread of leaves. Curled bronzed grubs, a couple of fat fronds are ready to uncoil.

Hazel wrinkles her nose. 'You sure?'

'She's hardly in any fit state to complain now.' Rose loads the fern onto the trolley with a grin.

Hazel shakes her head. 'Show some respect.' Her attempt to storm off is thwarted by the heavy trolley, and the narrowness of the long, leafy aisle. Rose grabs Rowan by the hand, and heads her sister off at the pass.

Hazel grips the handlebar of the trolley so hard that her knuckles whiten.

'Yes, I remember – happy now? I remember hiding in the feijoa bushes. And, if I'd known how they were going to set you off, I'd never have bought you those pineapple...fucking feijoas.'

'Fuck-fuck-fuckjoas.' Rowan swings from the handlebar like a chanting monkey. An elderly couple who've been checking out the hardy perennials take refuge in the gnomery.

Rose blocks Hazel's path. 'You are my sister. *You* were with me – so why say you didn't remember?'

'You act as though I choose what I remember.' Hazel folds her arms. 'I don't know why I can't remember what I can't remember.'

Rose tries to get eye-contact. 'Don't *want* to. That was *our* childhood that you say —'

'I don't *say*.' Hazel draws quote marks in the air. 'I *didn't* remember. And, I'm glad.'

'How can we be related? I can recall all of our childhood, and you were right there beside me. Claiming that you remember virtually nothing.' Rose shoves the trolley. 'And how long have you known that she's ill?'

Her sister stares at the ground, stubbing her sneaker against the path. 'That's not important.'

'Not for you – because *you* knew,' says Rose.

Rowan is watching them with a frown.

'Let's change the record.' Hazel gestures at Rowan.

'Anything for an easy life so.'

Hazel throws up her hands with a groan. 'What do you want for your misery – a parade?'

Rowan sits on the path. She yawns loud and long. 'Can I see the parade?'

Rose glares at her sister. 'Maybe you need some of that hypnotherapy, where they recover your memories for you.'

Hazel shakes her head. 'That's the whole point, Rose. I don't *want* to recover them.' She looks at her watch. 'It's time to go. I promised Mum that we wouldn't be long, and Rowan needs her nap.'

As Rose drives them back to her place, the silence is broken by Rowan singing. Hazel takes her time unloading the car, so Rose goes on ahead. She leaves the fern by the front door.

The house is strangely quiet. No television, no radio. No Vi.

'We're back,' she calls, as she fills the kettle. No-one answers.

She finds Vi on the sofa, cushions for a pillow, the throw draped over her cooling lower body. The dregs of her medication are on the coffee table beside her. She looks more peaceful than Rose ever saw her. The words drift through her mind, neither prayer nor blessing.

Blood and feijoas. The call of blood.

Rowan's shrill chicken-squawks in the hallway bring her to the present. Rose says goodbye, and draws up the rug until it covers her from head to toe.

She clucks to Rowan, turns her around and shepherds her outside again. Hazel is crouching down, watering the fern.

'She's – Mum's – g-o-n-e,' murmurs Rose.

'Yeah, I know.' Hazel gives a tight little sigh.

Rose takes Rowan to the nature reserve while Hazel waits for the funeral director. She pauses to study a meadow of pink marsh orchids, breathing in the woody scent of vegetation breaking down.

Rowan yawns and kicks her gumboots against the chicken-wire tread. 'And dinosaurs?'

'*And* monsters.' Rose checks her watch. 'All sorts of old things get preserved in a bog.'

Rowan grins.

They follow the silvering wooden boardwalk across the ancient bog, where the soil is a dark chocolate fudge. Rowan roars and staggers off, waving her arms, a toddler Frankenstein, her chestnut plaits bouncing against her head.

She comes to a sudden stop in the middle of the boardwalk, and points into the bog. 'What's that?'

Among the silver birch trees there's a plant almost two feet high. Inside a golden pyramid of last season's dead stalks, a lush umbrella of green fiddleheads is beaded with glistening crystals of dew. The central fronds are smaller, upright, dusted with rusty spores, but the longer branches arch elegantly towards the ground, forming a dense curtain.

'That's a royal fern,' says Rose.

'What's it mean?'

'Mean?' Rose slaps a feasting mosquito off her arm. 'It means King Osmund's fern. *Osmunda regalis*.'

'No,' moans Rowan. 'What does it *mean*? Mum says every plant's got a meaning.'

'Right.' Rose pilots her down the boardwalk. 'And, Rowan means?'

'Peace,' cries Rowan, tugging on her sleeve. 'And... Violet?'

'Violet? Modesty and innocence, apparently.'

'Nan-Vi says I'm precious.'

'Did she now?' Rose looks up; tracks a lone heron pulling herself through the sky.

Rowan nods, slow and definite; it's a fact not to be disputed. 'And – what does Loyal Vern mean?'

Rose hesitates. 'I'm not sure. I think it means healing.'

They wander on till they reach a wooden bench, worn smooth by the seasons.

Rose takes a seat. They watch the swaying sedges and lush reed beds, and listen to the warblers warbling. Rowan fidgets with her mittens, but for once she doesn't argue.

'Okay, once upon a time...'

'A long time ago?' says Rowan.

'Correct. There was a place called Loch Tyne where an old waterman – his name was Osmund – lived with his wife. And their very beautiful daughter.'

'Called Rowan.'

'Probably. And, from her light brown hair and rosy cheeks, you could tell that she came from Saxon roots. She ran light and fast as a young deer.'

Rowan nods and swings her legs. 'I run fast.'

'On late summer evenings, the girl often sat beside the lake with her mother to watch her father. He was working as a ferryman. As he crossed the lake, skimming deep blue waters, his oars would flash and drip. One day, they were watching Osmund when they heard footsteps hurrying towards them. Soon, a gang of men came out of the forest. They told the women that the cruel Danes were heading their way.'

Rowan leans closer against her arm.

'Within moments they could hear the Danes shouting. The gang of men were so frightened they ran back into the woods. Osmund grabbed his oars and began to row his wife and little daughter to a small island. Now, this island was covered by a big old fern. Osmund helped them off his boat, and then he guided them beneath the fern's drooping branches. And, that's where they lay and hid.'

'*Very* quietly,' says Rowan.

'*Very*, extremely quietly. Then, the ferryman rowed back across the water to his cottage. Just as he arrived, the group of Danes rushed in. Osmund was very scared at first, but they didn't hurt him...'

'He could row very fast,' says Rowan, waving her arms.

'That's right, so they knew that they needed him. And, for all the rest of that day and into the night, the Danes kept Osmund busy, ferrying troops of their fierce men backwards and forwards across the river. Once the last company of Danes was put on shore, Osmund kneeled on the ground and gave his thanks for his wife and child, who were still safely tucked away at the heart of the big fern on the little island.'

Rowan bites her bottom lip. 'They hid in the bushes, didn't they?'

'Uh-huh, right under the fern's branches.'

'Cool,' says Rowan.

'And years later, when she was a grown up, Osmund's daughter was reminded of that scary night, and how her father's quick thinking had saved them all. That's when she named that giant fern after him. And, from that day on, it was called *Osmunda regalis*. That's the royal fern. Alright?'

Rose watches a kestrel hovering, a crucifix in the sky. Banks of slate clouds are rolling in from the west. Thunder rumbles and Rowan grabs her hand.

'But, where's Vern?' Lightning flashes over a clump of gnarled oak trees on the edge of the bog, and the girl squeezes Rose's fingers tight.

'Who?' Rose checks her pocket for car keys.

Rowan splashes a mud puddle. 'Loyal Vern.'

'We'd better get home before the storm.'

Rowan's bottom lip quivers. 'But I want to look under the leaves for the hiding girl.'

'C'mon, it's only a silly old story, only made up. The sooner we go, the sooner we'll get home.'

In the back seat, Rowan stares out the window, waiting for Rose to fasten her car-seat.

'What are you thinking?' asks Rose.

'Nothing,' she sings, kicking her feet against the passenger seat.

'I can remember when I had time to think about nothing,' says Rose.

The girl turns to look at her. 'Loyal Vern.' She says. 'Read me that when we get home, Aunty Rose.'

Rose feels the blood rising to her face. The rash runs across her cheek, lumpy as Braille.

'Maybe. Or, we might try a new one. The old stories get boring after a while.'

GERALDINE MILLS

Geraldine Mills is a poet and fiction writer. She has had four collections of poetry and three of short stories published. She was awarded an Arts Council Bursary for *The Weight of Feathers* (Arlen House, 2007). She was a recipient of a Katherine Kavanagh Fellowship for her third poetry collection, *An Urgency of Stars* (Arlen House, 2010). Her short story collections have been taught at the University of Connecticut, Eastern Connecticut State University and Emerson College, Mass, USA summer programmes. She was the Millennium winner of the Hennessy/*Tribune* Emerging Fiction Award and the overall winner of the New Irish Writer Award for her story 'Lick of the Lizard'. The Arts Council awarded her a second bursary in September 2014 to work on short fiction. Her first children's novel, *Gold*, was published by Little Island in 2016.

The Naming of It

FLAME. SOOT. ASHES. BONES. Blocking my breath, suffocating me. I walk up and down the port, searching for the moon in the slow hollow of the night, pacing back and forth, too much erupting inside me to know any stillness. Cars drive up the ramp into the maw of the ferry, voices shout directions across at one another; there is the sickening smell of diesel. The staff let the foot passengers on. I wait my turn, wait for the people to move in front of me.

All chrome and steel, modern, mythical, this ferry sells the passengers an experience, with its themed restaurants, its cosy bucket seats, golden lighting. Fancy handbags hurry ahead of me, not wanting to catch my eye for fear they might see something of themselves reflected. I had a classy bag like that once, any amount of them, in fact, on the top shelf of the wardrobe, matching the outfit, the shoes.

The waiters in the café nod their heads in recognition as I order a tea, a sandwich. They have accepted me now, no longer ask why I take this trip back and over, back and over.

'Enjoy that,' they say.

I take the steps up into the open, making sure there is nothing but black firmament above my head, still the smell of burning, still a smoke ball catching at the back of my throat.

On deck I can breathe. The sky, so far above me, is big enough to push air into my lungs, to help me hold onto something inside me, always grateful for the wind on my face. I welcome it now as I do the sea-saw of the boat, its swell.

In the sheltered smoking area, diehards stand, pulling their coats around them, sunken-cheeked, puffing on their fixes. Even the presence of the red glint of tobacco is too much for me. I turn and head in the opposite direction. As far away from them as possible.

Keep the memories moving; keep them moving.

I pull the duffel coat more tightly around me. One-euro-fifty in a charity shop, grey with a hood and all its toggles intact that I found among the orphaned lids of Pyrex dishes, the ramble mix of saucers, the skirts and shirts with ghosts in their pockets. The woman volunteer said it was made for me. I looked at her but said nothing. It does its job, hides the smell of my own body. I'm no longer offended when people move away from me. I would have moved away from myself in my other life.

More passengers come up on deck, delight in their odyssey, holding onto the railings. Teenagers jostle and push one another, their arms stretched out, becoming the ship's figurehead. His DiCaprio to her Winslet, shouting out the well-known movie lines, laughing at the good of life, play-acting at jumping over the side, their screams as they pull one another back. Lovers, a tangle of arms and legs.

Lights coming into view – land. The commotion as the ferry docks and people start gathering their belongings. They all carry the lack of a good night's sleep in their bodies. Soon the dark is filled with the sound of trucks, cars pulling away, one following the other. A stream of foot passengers trudge towards the train, to be carried through England into the heaving world of industrial towns, the capital.

Before they have gone, bleary-eyed into the rush of sodium lights, the crew has already started cleaning the boat for the return journey. Great long brushes sweep up cups, half-bitten sandwiches, papers full of sick.

I stand by the concrete column covered in a flitter of posters, biding my time until they announce the return journey. I'm first in the queue to embark again, ashes and smoke still lodged there in the back of my throat. Orion overhead, the same constellation that used to shine over my own garden when I'd go out at night and bring in the washing off the line, clothes still full of pockets of fresh air, jeans stiff with frost. Hang them on the radiator, let them dry for the morning.

Keep the memories moving, keep them moving.

What of my neighbours back on my street, each side of the black holes of windows, charred doors? Do they give me a passing thought as they edge low-fat spread into the corners of their toast, or pick their noses as they leave for work? Tracy, the air hostess who whisks off with her wheelie bag; the world is still spinning for her. Never giving the house next door a second glance unless the rain unearths the smell of burning. Or Tim, who grows coleus plants from seed and has them in perfect rows all along his path. What of the bin lorry that chugs up the cul-de-sac, offloading the sleeping houses of their stinking rubbish?

Sometimes the tiredness is such that I fall asleep slouched over the railing until a baby's cry somewhere shatters me awake. Instinct makes me stretch out my hand to settle the fractious child, but all my fingers meet is the cold, damp metal. The cry won't let me go and I straighten up shivering, sit looking at the darkness, the cold unyielding.

There is more than one way for the soul to leave the body.

No matter what the night brings, I stay firm in my coat up on deck. The great vault of sky has changed to pitch and devil dark so that I can't read it, no sight of the moon to light the roof over my head. The tiny insistent voice still inside my heart. *Let go*, it whispers. *Let go.* But how can I?

A young man scrunched in a brown overcoat, a shine of dirt along the collar, the cuffs frayed, is sleeping against the hard frame of the boat. His eyes flicker under the lids and his chest rises and falls as if his breathing is carrying the rhythm of the vessel's movement. I watch him, the downturn of his lip, the yellowing of the skin around it,· his fingers still grasping the pint glass. His unsupported shoulder has a hump beneath the fabric. Then the growth moves towards his neck and a dark head emerges, followed by a slink of grey-brown fur and a long tail that sits on the coat's collar. Long, sharp, pink claws.

A rat.

The man shuffles and sits up. Awake now he takes a gulp from his pint of stout, rubs the cream froth from his lips and holds it out to the animal.

The rat licks the man's fingers.

I stare. Cannot help watching the rat rubbing against his fingers, the soft pink of its inner ear, the words the man is saying into it. Other than the staff in the café I have never spoken to anyone else on these crossings. But something about his gentleness makes me hunker down beside him.

'Can I touch it?' I say.

'She,' he says. 'Sal's a she, gentler than the Lamb of God Himself and more faithful. Aren't you, Sal?' He rubs his hand along the rodent's fur. 'Give me animals any day, they won't desert you, they'll stay with you to the bitter end.'

I feel the twist of knife in his words, try to shake it free. The rat looks up at me, quizzical, a tracery of drink-foam on its snout. My hand does what I ask it to do, tentatively stretches out and touches the fur. It's softer than I thought it would be, not coarse and wiry. By now I'm sitting down on the deck beside them.

'Does he go everywhere with you?'

The man nods. 'There's just me and Sal, killing the night. We sneak on when the crew's distracted. Across on the boat, see the lights of the city, the boats in the marina, turn around and back again. The air does us good and we're saved a night huddled in a doorway, isn't that right, Sal?' And he holds the animal closer to his cheek, her eyes flicker closed, then open again.

'Would you not be better off in a hostel?' I ask.

'I do that some nights, when I can smuggle herself in. The last one told me not to come back when they found her, said that there were enough vermin already. And he wasn't talking about rats. But we have our ways, don't we, Sal, to get around that.'

'How did you find her?'

'Well it was more like her finding me. A men's hostel in Battersea. She used to come scraping along the floor in the night and creep up onto the pillow. Just to stroke her fur helped me sleep when the pains in my legs were too bad. The pains got easier knowing she was there in the night. When all around me was shouting and hurling abuse at the night watchman, me and Sal just curled up in our bed and let no one be any the wiser. Once they spotted her creeping into my pocket that was the end of that. We have to be a bit creative. Don't we, Sal?' He leaned into her, looked across at me. 'What about yourself?'

'I could do with a cup of tea,' I say, easing myself up to standing. I'll knock these questions dead before they start.

'What happened to them?'

'What do you mean? Who?'

'The ghosts you're carrying around you.'

I shiver in my rat-grey coat, look back across at him.

'When you've lived like me you get to read people.'

His eyes hold mine. They have the sheen of listening in them. Of trustworthiness. Why I tell him I don't know, but he keeps my gaze until I push the first word out, then stop, then start again, trying to find a way. Choke on them, spit them out, struggle to find the road back to that morning.

Martin had insisted that I go away for the night with my friend.

You sure? I had replied, turning from my laptop to look at him.

What do you take me for? A complete idiot? He had said, accusing me of thinking that just because he didn't have a high-flying job like me that he couldn't look after our son. I tried to backtrack, saying that it wasn't what I meant, but he was hurt. I wished I could have taken back the tone in my voice. But the idea of a break was so tempting. Work was particularly fraught, a manager that was bordering on a bully; Martin moping around, still no job, still not doing anything about it, and me wondering how long I could put up with that.

 'I told him it would probably be the last time anyway because once he got back on his feet there wouldn't be a minute. Then I kissed the top of his head as if he was a little boy, kissed the top of the other precious head, my darling boy.'

'What was your little boy called?'

I turn away from him, look up at the moon that's moving in and out through the clouds as the ferry eats through the water. I wish that the man up there would come down and lie beside me. Let his silver thighs wrap themselves around me, my belly fill up with him, make me forget. Make me believe in the cold life of him.

'Can you not say it?' Though his hands are stroking the rat, his attention is still on me. Reading me.

'Paul.' It jumps out before I can stop it. 'An old family name on my father's side.'

'What happened?' His voice is as quiet as a radio with the sound turned down low.

Martin was so keen that I go. It was the most upbeat I had seen him in weeks. I went with his blessing. Off with an old friend I hadn't spoken to in years, until the request on Facebook. A whim, a fancy. The messages whizzing back and forth. Yes, I would stay overnight, seizing the day, the night and all that. The baby sitting up on his high chair, his mouth all orange from too much carrot purée, spitting it onto my angora cardigan so I had to change once again before I headed out the door. I hugged them a second time, and a third before I stepped into the car and drove to the hotel. One of those boutique ones, candles in nooks, a smooth Rioja, Carpaccio, *Iles flottantes*.

The friend, Myra, hadn't changed, still held herself very well. Her hair, her makeup, so few lines on her forehead that I had to look for the telltale shine of botox. It didn't seem to be there at all, while I had to keep checking my own shoulder to make sure there wasn't a little deposit of sick that I had forgotten about.

She had never married, had one pregnancy that she had got rid of and had never regretted. I filled in my own life, told her how I had married late, a miracle of a child, my husband Martin. They were everything to me.

And as I was talking to her, I knew it had been a mistake to have come. I had nothing in common with this not-a-hair-out-of-place woman who sat before me. I had been thinking I was missing out, when all my riches were at home.

I was too old for girlie nights. I would leave immediately next morning.

I stopped, trying to catch my breath, scrabbling for the courage to let it out: how my phone started ringing in the middle of darkness of a strange hotel room, not knowing where I was when it woke me. Only the panic, driving roads that gave me no leeway. Praying, praying. Please God, not this. The smoke billowing out the windows, the crackle of rafters as they split and flamed down. Screaming to be allowed through. Tough arms holding me back. How easily two lives can be snuffed out.

Flame.

Soot.

Ashes and Bones.

Ashesandbones.

'And that was that,' I say.

The man says nothing for a while, keeps rubbing Sal's ears.

'Just because it's home, doesn't mean it's safe,' he says.

I look out across the deck, wait for each of those words to find the knowing place inside me. Sal has buried herself into the crook of his arm as if she can't bear to be away from him.

I let the memory in. The night before I left, all around our house the light had been sucked out of the land and left a glow that softened the dark measures of winter. Martin didn't want me to switch on the light. Instead I lit candles, six of them steady and true reflected in the window-pane beyond us. The fire threw its heat out into the room and there was little sound but our talking, the baby's even breath coming through the monitor.

My heart shudders. Before it starts to sunder, I stand up and move around, my legs now stiff from sitting too long on the hard ground. Walking up and down, the life slowly comes back into them.

'I'll get us that cup of tea now.' I say. 'And something for Sal?'

'Chipsticks. She loves Chipsticks.'

I make my way upstairs to the café. Above me, the moon has chosen to show its face. It builds a glistening road across the sea, strong enough for any disbeliever to walk on.

I order two cups of tea, sandwiches, the packet of Chipsticks. There is the hiss of boiling water into the paper cups, the tea bag floating. Waiting for my change, the night comes back to me again. How we cooked, brought our meal in beside the fire, reminding ourselves of what we had and what we couldn't lose no matter what, as we lay together on the couch. A silver moon shone through the windows and covered us then, too. The clear frosty sky with its own stars took all the night away and I wanted to go walking in it but Martin's perfect warmth beside me held me.

I pick up the brown paper bag with my purchases, head back to the man and his companion. The tiniest flicker of burden falls from my shoulders. The letting out of pain. The listening. The naming of it.

EOIN DOLAN LANE

Eoin Dolan Lane was a finalist in the 2016 Irish Writers Centre Greenbean Novel Fair for *In the Shadow of Hermes*. He was also the fourth prize winner in the inaugural year of the RTÉ Frances MacManus Short Story Competition 1986, when James Plunkett was the head judge (the story was later published in the accompanying anthology by Mercier Press). In 2015, Eoin was shortlisted in the same awards for his story 'When Blue Snowflakes Fall'. *Beyond the Horizon* is Eoin's second novel.

When Blue Snowflakes Fall

If I clench my toes I can hear them say my name.

When I clasp my knuckles tight until the bones protrude, I can sense the name around me. But it is not within me. It is not of me and I cannot say my name. When their faces bend over me, I hear the name on their lips like snowflakes about to fall across the bed. I cannot remember my name. They say my name is Annelise and the sound of my name comes to me as a light flurry of snow settling on my face.

My cheeks are hot and flushed and my name lands and melts on my cheeks. A beautiful name, I think. Annelise. But I do not remember being Annelise. Loose strings fiddle around in my head like notes in the wrong place. I cannot seem to place them in any order. I cannot finish the jigsaw.

The nurse is leaning over me and whispering.

There is a man, with a bald head like an egg smiling at me.

He says he is my husband.

I do not remember having a husband. I remember sometimes a man in the background reading the paper, when I was working.

I am a painter. I do not remember being a painter. I do not remember painting. I know because they have told me so.

There are paintings all around this room. They have brought them here. But I do not know these paintings. They stare at me in the dark when I try to sleep and I wish someone would take away my paintings.

'Take away my paintings,' I want to say.

Please.

Take.

Away.

I do not recognise my own paintings. But in the night, in the small hours when I sail silently through the hours, I sense things. These are my new paintings. Perhaps there is something of me left in me still, if even only in the small hours when I sail through the night.

I sail on waters of blue. There are anemones, sea anemones floating deep down under the water which is cut like crystal, sparkling and splintering as if a shoal of mackerel is flittering through the strong current to the nether regions which only divers and fish can reach. I am sailing in this foil of blue with the sun streaking through my skin; my entire being is infused like a watercolour in shades and tones of blue.

The paintings around the bed are blue. Cerulean and aquamarine and azure with shades of ink and Himalayan poppy blue and they are ringed around the bed like prompt cards urging me to remember. But perhaps I do not want to remember.

They have brought me to this place, to this room and they have brought my paintings here as to a gallery. As if this were some sort of exhibition.

They say I will get better.

The nurse says I was upset. She says I must rest.

The man smiles at me. He comes in the afternoons and brings me flowers.

But I do not know these people and I exist in this bed as on a desert island surrounded by seas of blue paintings.

And I swim in my mind in the sea. I glide and coil like an eel through clear water. My body is weightless and I swim in smooth curving spirals through rainbows of blue, my arms slicing the water without sound, my legs and feet fluttering in my slipstream and I am away for hours like this in my mind, in the water just curling along, like a submarine with no destination, with no land in sight and no need to turn back.

And sometimes I swim through the bones. I am swimming through bundles of bones and they knock and bump against my limbs. And now, I lie in this bed and I sense the grey bones. I am the bundle of bones. My bones are grey and they float as if bobbing in water. I have been trying to swim past my bones, my own remains. What remains of me floats between these sheets, levitates on these sheets, suspended, lifeless, vacant and staring into space and I am reduced to this grey bundle of bones in this room.

The nurse comes and says I was sleeping. She is tucking the sheets around me, burying my bones as in a shroud. She tucks my bones in and the man comes.

The man is smiling. He is bending over the bed and he has brought flowers. I look at the bunch of flowers and I see seaweed. I see the smooth, black stems of seaweed hovering over the bed as if threatening to choke me, entangle me in their slick, slimy fingers.

The man with the head like an egg is smiling at me.

And his smile is like lightning flashing in a rainstorm. There is thunder gathering and the clouds are wrestling in the sky, on the ceiling, collapsing over the bed and the thunder snaps. His smile ignites the room like a serpent spitting venom, like forked lightning striking a dead tree.

The noise is rising now. The volume is turned up full blast. Plates are being smashed, twirling off shelves as if by themselves.

A woman is turning around and each way she turns, she sees plates and cups flying off shelves, smashing to the floor, cracking into jigsaws of blue. The curtains are wrenched from the windows and the blue gauze curtains are draped around her head and she is entwined in a veil of blue and she is storming around, swathed in gauze and she can hear crying, shrieking in every corner, in every room and everywhere she runs, the screaming greets her, for the screaming is coming from within.

Her fingers are growing; they are growing into branches; they are paintbrushes and she is swirling against the walls, dragging her fingernail brushes in swooping arcs and heaves and she is smearing the walls with anger and with rage and she is painting in vicious stabbing circles of blue.

'I am leaving tonight,' he said.
   'I have brought you some roses,' he says.
'I am leaving you for her,' he said.
   'They have no scent,' he says.
'I don't want to hurt you,' he said.
   'I will put them in water,' he says.
'I never meant to hurt you,' he said.
   'The nurse says you should sleep now,' he says.

I remember snippets of things. Feelings and moments. I do not remember the rest of him, the rest of us. The bits before this strange room where I lie dulled and confused.

But I can feel him leaving this room now. He is leaving me with his bunch of unscented roses. And he leaves me with my blue paintings and the nurse who will look in on me. I lie alone again. It is like being raped by pirates and held captive in a strange place.

'What does she look like? What does she look like? What does she look like?' I said.
   'Where did you meet? Where did you meet? Where did you meet?' I said.

'What's her name? What's her name? What's her name?' I said.

A noise grinds. It is his car driving away. It grinds in my head and in my ears and I turn my face to the pillows to block out those tyres from my head.

The sound of him driving away. That night and this afternoon. To that other woman.

A woman I cannot even name.

The very thought of him touching other limbs such as mine blanks my mind.

I am numb. I am bones and I am locked in this bed.

The nurse is the only other woman I know now and she is more like a nun or a maiden aunt than a flesh and blood woman. She comes softly in white, speaking quietly and sometimes I even think she cares about me a little. She has no real smell and if she emits any odour it is of antiseptic and medicine and powder.

I yearn for a blue bird to sing while I lie here, inoculated with the noise of his tyres on the gravel outside and I wait in what seems like vain hope for the blue bird to sing.

It is snowing now and I am standing on a frozen beach playing ducks and drakes, skimming the pebbles across the icy waves.

And here comes that sound again. Here comes the sound, the very low, faint hissing sound of cell splitting cell, of hairs cracking away; the sound of skin tearing apart.

A woman is ripping her arms. She is wandering barefoot through the garden, fondling her arms in the thorns of roses. She is breathing deep and fast and she is coming into the house stark naked, her white skin like marble, her veins outlined in tributaries of blue and wandering around like a drunken statue about to topple and crash into smithereens on the floor.

They say they found me on the floor.

They say I had cut myself. The nurse says I had suffered a shock.

But I can hear the blue bird singing.

The blue bird has come now and the snowflakes fall again and I feel them settling on the bed, covering my arms and my cheeks and they are nestling in my hair while the blue bird sings. And the song trembles and quivers and the hairs on my arms shiver with the song and the rush of blue snowflakes falling from the ceiling.

And I am quiet in the song. I am wet through with the moisture of soft snowflakes. I rise quietly and go about my task silently. There is no rage here; there is nothing but the sweet song of the blue bird singing in my ears and I begin to paint again. I paint the patterns of snowflakes on the walls. And I draw from my rivers of blue, from the tributaries of blue down my arms, like mountain springs trickling through snow. I paint patterns of streams on the walls. I paint in swirls and arcs and curves like a swimmer gliding through and all the while hearing nothing but the blue bird trilling from on high and from deep down within.

When the door opens, I carry on.

When the nurse speaks, I do not hear her at first.

When she grabs me in her arms, I notice her like a boat on the river.

'Annelise,' she says. 'Annelise.'

I smile at her through the snowflakes. They are falling on her shoulders and she is becoming blurred in the storm. She is fading fast.

'Annelise,' she says. 'You are covered in blood. The walls are covered in blood.'

I smile at her. 'I wanted to paint the rivers,' I say. 'I wanted to paint the rivers in my arms. I wanted to paint the blue rivers.'

She is wrapping fabric around my arms. And I stare at my arms. The rivers are plugged now and the blue waters are stilled.

She bends her face closer to me and she hugs me in her arms.

'Can you tell me your name?' she says softly. 'Can you say your own name?'

I look at her and nod. The nurse holds me and waits.

I take a deep breath and the blue snowflakes fall on my hair and on my shoulders and I say, 'Yes.'

I lean closer to her and I say my name.

I whisper my name into her ear.

'My name,' I say, 'is Blue.'

COLIN BARRETT

Colin Barrett is from Mayo, Ireland. His first book, *Young Skins*, was published in 2013. His writing has appeared in the *New Yorker*, *Granta*, *The Guardian* and *The Stinging Fly* magazine.

The Cold God of Bad Luck

Because all humans are imperfect, even the most consumingly selfish person is only imperfectly so. Lorna Dawes' consuming selfishness was her defining – at times it felt like her only – feature, but there were those periods when her selfishness seemed to exhaust itself and lapse into a kind of dormancy. It was in such periods that Lorna found herself susceptible to the plight of others. And who, exactly, were the others? Oh, all of them, that sprawling mass of humanity, eight billion or so of the suckers, dozens of whom she could count as personal acquaintances, or better. This latter group, with their sticky particularities and uncanny ability to relentlessly conspire against their own best interests, proved harder to be moved by. Take the mother, for instance, or take the father, for instance, but let's not even, with either, because where to start? Anyhow, both were safely sequestered back in Lorna's hometown, a dismal provincial fixture in the west of Ireland best known as the site of a former nun-run Mother and Baby home where, from the nineteen-twenties through to the fifties, the little bodies of the children who died in the nuns' care were stuffed, as a matter of course, into a septic hole in a far field off the premises.

Lorna was thirty-one years old, and lived in Dublin. She worked in the support centre for an online betting company. Her job was to contact those customers whose accounts had fallen into arrears. It was an easy gig because gamblers, or Irish gamblers at any rate, were a uniformly cringing and suppliant species of loser: theirs was the cosmological resignation of the loser who believes his loserdom is intrinsic and inescapable, and the call from Lorna was to them a relieving affirmation of this belief, like a call from The Cold God of Bad Luck herself. Because Lorna was a consumingly selfish person, she had no sympathy for these sad, invariably male voices as they blubbed, wheedled and bargained into her ear.

On her lunch break, she ate avocado sandwiches on the fifteenth floor rooftop smoking area of her building and watched the slow, delicate work of the cranes dotted throughout the industrial estate skyline, their hooked lines patiently rising and sinking between the skeletons of the unfinished structures. The cranes made her think of keyhole surgery. She had worked all over Ireland in her twenties, pinging from one zero hour gig to another – PA, data entrist, secretary, call centre rep – and was a member of what her younger brother Robert informed her was called the precariat. When he began explaining what the term precariat meant – she said, 'yeah, yeah, Bo, I get it.'

Robert – or Bo, as he was now known – was twenty-three, and had moved to Dublin last year for a second stab at art college, his manic depression having ruined his first go round in Galway. Because Lorna was a consumingly selfish person, she had arranged the terms of her life in such a way as to have remained ignorant of just how bad things had gotten for Robert in Galway, and she felt determined now to overcome her instinct towards self-protection in order to properly support her brother. But the truth was that Robert was another person Lorna found it easier to love when he was a confounding, guilt-generating absence. In person, it usually took about fifteen minutes before she wanted to push him over the nearest low wall. Take, for example, the preposterous diminutive – Bo! – he wished to be known by. Not Rob or Bob or Bobby, but Bo! It was barely a noise, and of course all his art college friends were delighted to accede to Robert's whim. It had taken a gruelling degree of self-control for Lorna to resist asking them to call her 'Lo'.

Lorna went out with Bo and his friends every week. Bo's friends affected to be delighted by Lorna, but she knew what they were delighted by was her bitterly prideful insistence on standing them drinks. They were students and aspiring artists, and they were, in fairness, poor, though most of them were poor in the way that people who can move back into the homes of their middle-income-or-better parents whenever they wanted were poor. She bought them drinks and they talked with high passion and enviable articulacy of the opacity of process, of something called postmortem-neoliberalism, how shit Hozier was. Lorna went drinking with them every Thursday, and every second Sunday attended AA. AA was good because it was a place where Lorna could admit to the true scale and scope of her selfishness, though she was aware that these denunciations of her selfishness, no matter how thorough and unsparing, were ultimately just one more function of it. Still, she used AA to regularly perform a searching and fearless moral inventory of herself, and always came to the same conclusion: she had never, in any way, made anyone's life better.

She went to art shows with Bo and his friends. Bo drank copiously at them. He drank all the complimentary booze he could get his hands on and carried a naggin of Tallisker around in his coat pocket for maintenance purposes. An artist at one of the shows had a speech impediment and Bo went up to the man and stared at him until the man was obliged to interrupt the small monologue he was delivering to a crowd of absorbed patrons to ask Bo, what, exactly, was his problem. *Ttpph*, Bo said, then *Ttpph* again, then finally he roared, *TTTHHUFERRING TTTHUCKATHHHAGE.*

Or he did his Jack Nicholson Joker bit, prancing past a row of installations and handwaving at each work, rolling his Rs, saying CRRRAP, CRRRAP, CRRRAP, CRRRAP, until arbitrarily pausing at one piece, turning to Lorna and his friends, his top lip satyrishly curled just like Nicholson's Joker, and saying, 'Now that's good work.'

Just to rile him Lorna told him all art was nonsense and he said, sure don't I know.

'Your friends are posturing fakes,' she told him and he said, 'sure don't I know.'

'But I like them anyway,' she conceded, and he said, 'sure don't I know.'

Every six months Lorna spent a weekend back home. The mother and the father were no longer together, though their relationship had sunk into a very Irish kind of purgatory. The father had moved out, but only as far as the granny flat at the bottom of the garden. There, the father could drink until he vomited in peace, thirty yards from the back door of the kitchen, and he and the mother had agreed set times of the day for taking turf from the turf shed, so their paths would not cross. Sometimes, rinsing a plate in the sink, Lorna would glimpse the spectral smudge of the father's profile in the little kitchen window of the granny flat. Like most men his age, he was domestically incompetent, and after thirty years of marriage bare-ly knew how to boil an egg. Lorna's suspicion was the mother still cooked his dinners and left them at his door, though the mother never admitted to this. Certainly, whenever Lorna found the stamina to spend half an hour in the flat, enduring the excruciating near-silence that constituted a conversation with her father, he moved about the cramped kitchen fixtures with the baffled tentativeness of a stroke survivor. She sometimes wondered if her father *had* suffered a stroke, and nobody had bothered to tell her. Because she was a consumingly selfish person, she only ever felt relief when she left the flat.

Her mother made Lorna come on walks with her, long treks down country lanes, no matter the weather. The last time they'd gone, the sun was shining and it was pouring down, because this was how the weather in the west frequently occurred: all at once. As they went along, the mother listed off the various small ways in which her friends had failed and betrayed her over the last few months – the mother was a great one for making a searching and fearless moral inventory of other people. The puddles in the ruts of the lane were burning mirrors. Lorna was wet and warm. There was a herd of Friesians sitting in a field, a sheen to the slopes of their haunches that made them look like wet rock.

Lorna asked her mother if she and the father were going to getting a divorce.

'We are not getting a divorce,' the mother said.

'But you are separated.'

'We are not separated,' the mother said.

'But you don't live together anymore.'

'But we do,' the mother said.

'But you don't,' Lorna said. 'It's over.'

'In a way,' the mother said.

'In what way? If it's not over then what is it?'

'It is what it is,' the mother said.

The only thing either parent asked her about Dublin was how the job was going, though they had long ago given up on bothering to keep track of what her current job was, as most of Lorna's positions lasted less than a year and they all seemed fairly interchangeable, which they were.

Lorna wasn't sure how often Bo came home. He disappeared most weekends in Dublin, but Lorna doubted he was making the pilgrimage west any more regularly than she. There was a girl among his set, Emma, with pageboy hair and the beguiling pallor of someone with a chronic blood disorder, and it was Lorna's suspicion that she and Bo had something. Lorna could not be sure, and it was futile to ask, but she had observed the silence, like a kind of loyalty, with which Emma listened in the pub whenever Bo was speaking, even when what he was saying was absolute garbage. Because she was a consumingly selfish person, Lorna hoped it was true.

In the industrial estate the cranes multiplied and the buildings grew, the tramline route from the city centre was extended further out, and investigating officials at the Mother and Baby home were still hauling remains out of the ground, still counting out the bones. There were days when Lorna's malign selfishness was so acute she felt like she couldn't breathe for all the unbearable weight of herself upon herself, and she had to lock her body into a toilet cubicle and drop her head between her knees until her throat eased back open.

One day, she rang her father from work. The calls out were on an automatic dialler. She asked to speak to Mr. Dawes and didn't realise it was her father until he spoke. She had not yet given him her name, and didn't: he didn't seem to know it was her. His account was 91 euros in arrears going back several months. Lorna explained this to him and he still didn't recognize her. It was just after midday, and there was a liquored slur to his voice, which had turned as grave and small as all the other losers' voices. She told him she could accept an immediate payment by credit card and if he could not supply that she would have to bar his account until he paid the outstanding sum, plus a penalty, by card, postal order, or cheque.

There was silence on the line as the father absorbed this info.

'Do you have any dependents?' Lorna asked him, though such a question was of course not part of the protocol.

'Dependents?'

'Yes, like children?' she asked.

After another long silence, he said, 'no, it's just me here.'

'Well that's a shame,' she said. 'And now, Mr Dawes, for the last time, I have to ask you to tell me how it is you wish to pay.'

R.M. CLARKE

R.M. Clarke began her career as an actress in 2006, moving behind the scenes into voiceover work and writing some years later. Her short stories have been published in *Losslit*, *The Open Pen Anthology* and Dublin 2020, and she is a contributing writer to writing.ie. Her debut novel, *The Glass Door*, won the 'Discovery' award at the Dalkey Book Festival and The Irish Writers Centre Greenbean Novel Fair 2016. She lives in Dublin, where she volunteers as an outreach speaker for the Rape Crisis Centre.

The Letter

The man in the other car had been a priest. The word was he'd taken a drink before he got behind the wheel and the investigation after proved the word to be true. But it was the cigarette that had caused him to swerve. He'd thrown it out the window once it was dragged but the wind had pushed it back. Then the cigarette took on the habit, set fire to it at the lap. It was then he had drifted across the line and into my father's car headlong and pushed him off the mountain road.

It was decided after a time that it was less the fault of the man himself than it was simple bad luck, or that it had been decided in some way. A small chain of events – the drink, the car, the cigarette, the gust of wind, the fire – led to the thing itself: the two cars colliding, my father's coming off worse, the road high and without boundary, the fall steep and far. It was never said out loud but it was heard and known all the same; it became common thought that the priest's life had been spared and our father's life taken by the hand of God.

Here now, far and long away from there and then, the sun is coming up and the heat is already rising from the hard earth. Soon the blue sky will glare down at me. It is nothing like the wet green bearing in of home. I pause above the page, now taken up a quarter with the black scrawls of my hand, waiting for the next words to come. I know I am out of date with this form. I could as easily write a text, send an email. But this seems right, this pen and ink. I have long been out of time with you, as I am almost with myself. I've not talked to you for years, years you've not been able to chip away at the silence I've built up between us with distance. And yet here we are.

The spasm catches me across the chest and I am shocked into stillness. I have known these often now but each time it takes my breath. I wonder when the end comes if it will go like that, the seizing striking out of nowhere and then the darkness.

Anyway. Pen to the page.

I was seven, then. You were twelve. Every Saturday my father and I used to head out to the football ground. He was a soccer player by trade, do you remember that? You must. A midfielder for the Dublin Wanderers. It didn't fit him afterwards, somehow. Dying young in that position didn't seem right, that sort of fast burning out was usually reserved for a striker. But it happened all the same. He died just as easily and impossibly as anyone else. There and then not there, the cruel and simple and true of it.

I used wait for Saturday mornings with a giddy joy, laying out my clean kit the night before to mirror his so I could jump into it in the morning and be down at the breakfast table before him, waiting for his words to come booming down the staircase:

Oh it's a fine old day to be a Wan-Der-ER!

And when he came into the kitchen, with the breakfast things already laid out by Mam, he'd pause by the door and look at me, his eyes glinting.

What kind of day is it today, Frankie?

it's a fine old day to be a wan-der-er!

Never a truer word spoken my lad.

And then he'd lay into the toast and eggs Mam had made him with a savagery and she would pour the tea and sit at last and spoon out big gel blobs of marmalade onto her own toast and mine while you and Jamzie slept. She used to watch his games, had met him at a game there when he was on the juniors, but now there were five of us including us three children and there were always things to do. I was the family rep, week in week out I was there beside him in the car as we drove over the mountains from Rathfarnham, watching the city spill out before us and the buildings cluster ever tighter together as we reached the field, there beside him on the pitch in the team box, roaring with the rest of them. The team used to call me Frankie the Manager. Da loved that. You and Jamzie never came. You were twelve then and he was fourteen and you had things to do, like Mam, schoolwork to finish and your friends to walk to the shops with and Jamzie had girls to look after and places to go on his bike. So it was just me and Da on Saturdays.

I called him Da when I was young. It was only afterwards, maybe years after – when I no longer retraced the Saturday car journey over the mountains in my mind – that he became my father. I had known him all my life when he died, until my years of living long eclipsed the time we'd shared. And then he was as unknown as a stranger, and as bizarre and remote and formal. Then he was my father. I knew you much longer.

I had fallen ill after the game the week before, and the fever rose in me suddenly and severely. The rain had fallen without relent on the pitch, had been falling all morning, and though Mam had tried to keep me in the house I had refused. The next day I couldn't move and was left off school all week, groaning into myself as that Saturday came ever closer. Game day. I had never missed one.

The night before I willed myself into wellness. I don't think you knew how hard I did as you sat with me bent over your schoolwork, rising from it now and then to put a hand to my cheek and urge the broth to my mouth while dinner was being cooked downstairs. I didn't want to be stuck there the next day while Da did his drive over the mountains without me, while he fought on the pitch for ninety minutes without me roaring him on, or started the car up without me on the way home, stopping in for ice cream if it was a hot day, penny sweets if it was a cold. The sheets clung to my hot limbs and I had stern words with them in his voice to cool down, to dry up, to become light and mobile, to be better by morning. When darkness came and I rose briefly out of a thick sleep, you and your books had left but I could hear you through the wall that separated your room from mine, your feet doing a soft shoe on the wooden boards, the low hum of the radio and your voice. The darkness fell over me then and I saw the faces of angels at the windows. I saw the captain of the Dublin Wanderers, the centre-forward Timmy Murphy, who had legs like lightning bolts and was my hero; I saw my father's laughing mouth of teeth; I saw you. You were reaching out to me with your hand, as though asking me to dance. All of you were calling to me as though your voices were strings attached to my chest and pulling me onwards to you. The sleep that came then was deep and fitful and in the morning I was cold and heavy as sand.

His stomping chant woke me, echoing up through the floorboards and creeping into my sleep like a long forgotten thing suddenly remembered.

It's a fine old day to be a WAN-DER-ER!

And when the kitchen echoed in silence the noise of him reversed and the booming of his steps came back up the stairs and burst into my bedroom.

Against the window the raindrops made a series of rapid rippling pools, swinging me forcibly from a lying down position to the twisted depth of a sediment bed beneath a body of clear water. I sunk down as he spoke, each pooling drop further and further above the closing darkness. I fought to wake for him and when I finally did he was gone. Whatever his words were that he had spoken to me last had gone with him.

Mam swung through the door after a time and laid her hard cold hand on my forehead where last yours had been and whispered about getting the shopping and went. Then the house settled. It, like the rest of us, did not know what was to come. Sleep fell on me again until I heard you.

It wasn't your voice at first. It was your feet, scuffling along the wood of the room next door, the big room you had to yourself as the only girl, the room Jamzie coveted and fought you over. At first, through the heavy state I was under, I thought you might have been dancing. Then I heard your voice.

No.

There was a laugh in it, but the laugh sat atop a deeper pull, like a blob of oil on a body of water. The laugh was not your own. Then there was silence, and then you said it again, and then the floorboards creaked under weight and then I heard Jamzie.

You did it the last time and you liked it.

I did not know what he meant then but it was the way the words were said.

The scuffling started up again, violent and subdued and then it ceased, and I heard the sheets being worried, the springs of the bed being put under oath. And that word again. No. Over and again, so gentle as to almost not be heard, like a prayer learned by rote but never understood.

Silence came again, and I found that the sheets clung to me in every crevice and that my face was hot and wet and sore from where my jaw had been held shut. My ears were so locked on the movement through the wall that I did not hear the bedroom door, did not see Jamzie standing there watching me. When I turned and saw him a shudder came over me and he smiled.

Feeling better now Frankie?

I stared at him, but could not move my head and he looked me full in the face with eyes that were empty of knowing. And it might have been something else I thought then, a misunderstanding, something that I could never know. Perhaps you and Jamzie, who were so much older and schooled and busy with your lives and friends outside of home and knew things that I could not, inhabited a place where words had different meanings, where they were not meant fully or the same. They might be given with a laugh that was believed even though it seemed false, or was only incidental, or their repetitions might be like a song to be sung along to because it has been heard so often it rises from you without effort. Perhaps this place was where a series of small and blameless events would latch on to one another and lead, without intention, to the thing itself, the thing it was that brought a word from you that was at once incontestable and meaningless, and I could not understand that and no one could be held responsible. And after all I was sick.

Jamzie watched me and his empty eyes filled up at last with something like satisfaction, like understanding.

I'll bring you up a thing to drink, you look bothered.

He kept his eyes on me as he pulled the door over. At last it closed on him and the room next door held its breath. And it was like when you look at the wood of the wardrobe doors and see a face where before it was just the lifeless incidentals of the woodgrain, you can never after unsee that face, you can never after unknow that the wardrobe lives. And every time your eyes were downcast or your shoulders rounded I wondered if it had happened again. The thing that drew that no. And though for years I did not know what that thing was I came to know in time, when words like Da got elbowed out of my mouth by Father, and made space for things I had never before understood. And every time Jamzie brushed past you in the kitchen and you went still and every time he looked at me full in the face with empty eyes I knew I would die if I ever found the words for a thing I couldn't speak. And that same afternoon when everything changed for all of us in the same levelling way, when the phone rang at tea and Mam came into the kitchen as though her entire body had been drawn of blood and we all had to sit and accept the simple chain of events that led to the thing itself, what space did that leave any of us in which to speak and be heard?

The other driver – whose fault it wasn't at all, an accident after all just an accident and accidents happen – the priest, insisted on leading the ceremony for us and Mam couldn't say no, or if she had said it, he hadn't heard. When he stood at the bow of the church before us, his loose neck wobbled every time he said our father's name. Jonathan. It was the way he held the final 'n' at the back of his throat long after his mouth had stopped working. The sound lingered and insinuated itself into the echoes and lasted. You sat on my right side and were so still it seemed you held your breath. Jonathann. And his throat skin was

like an old shirt left on the line in the wet. And Jamzie
was on my left and though he didn't move or speak I
could feel him stretching out over me towards you like
a shadow. Jonathannn. Our mother had always called
him Jonny. In the Wanderers he was Jonny Gorman
the Number 4 Man. Timmy Murphy, my hero of the
lightning legs, had called him Johnboy. I knew him
as Da. There was no Jonathan except in the church
suffocated in the throat of that priest.

At the end of the ceremony he came straight over
to us to take our hands in his in turn and to hold at
last to our mother's.

It's been a horrible confusion of events, he said.

After, our aunt Margaret passed a plate of
sandwiches to my mother in the kitchen and said:

It could have been worse, Celeste. He could have
knocked the priest off the road himself.

I saw my mother's face then as I had never seen
it before. It was a look that hardened itself into the
ridges and deeps of her cheeks, and around her mouth
and nose. A pulling down and sharpening. That face,
the one I didn't know, stayed with her through the
next years of work and the worrying you into the
housework and the cooking, the time when you gave
up on all the things you did and dreamed, your youth,
your time with friends, your schooling. It stayed with
her and hardened her sight against all things, against
what you needed her to see, against what she saw
herself. And I'm talking about Jamzie, you know that.
Jamzie and how he was and who he was and how he
moved around you. How he would brush past you in

the kitchen, bend over you too close when you were making tea or filling a glass at the sink. The way his eyes followed your hips. It stayed with her through all of that until she found her way into our father's plot five years later.

The spasm catches me across the chest again and I hold myself still until it breathes through. They come so often now I wonder if I imagine them. I don't know why I am writing these things down, stories I have told and stories I have never spoken, but there is something in this that is necessary, now. Because it has lain still and unbreathing beneath many layers of dirt and water, beneath many stagnant breaths. And though I knew it was there after that day I never again looked for a face in the wood grain. In the silence of the night I slept with my head under the pillow and breathed loud through my mouth and turned obnoxiously and sometimes I hummed until my ears were filled and it felt again that I was under water where nothing could touch me or anyone else.

Because the thing was, you loved us. All of us. But you loved me most, and I couldn't have that change. And after our father died and Mam had to take on work, you did all that was asked of you and you turned it at last into an art. You grew in love when there seemed nothing left worth loving in any of us. On Sundays you boiled a great pink ham for the week and I used watch it steam on the side as it cooled, my mouth aching for it. You made our sandwiches for the next day in order of age and kept mine for last. I sat with you and watched while Mam and Jamzie watched the telly next door, and we were left to our softness and our quiet. You kept the best bits back for my sandwich and buttered both slices of bread on the inside, and only we knew. You did the mustard lightly all over the ham so that it touched every surface of the meat without piling up too much in one place, because it was the piling up that caused the sting. You slapped it thick on Jamzie's in great lumps and we both smiled while you did it though neither of us said why. I cried and cried when you finally got out and left us and married Brian.

Manuela from next door is out already, sweeping. Over here, they keep their places spotless. Each few square metres of path is claimed and kept, swept each morning without fail or regret. The sound grates and soothes at once, like nails against skin on fire with itching. She drags the brush, today as every day, to the corner of the path above the gutter and raps out the head with three short sharp strikes, loosening the stale dirt through the grates. She looks over at me where I sit above these few pages watching her stiffly as though caught in a wrongdoing.

She calls brightly up to me.

Hola señor! Te sientes mejor?

Si, un poco.

I smile so easily through the untruth and bend again over this page. I hear her heavy steps move back indoors. It was always so easy to conserve, to play small, to hold back. We learned it young. Carol says it's my way of punishing myself. She has been taking care of everything these past few months, the doctors, the paperwork that goes with being an expat in a hard-earthed land you've never once learned to navigate with ease. She has made herself indispensable.

The sun is rising to its fullness and the heat is beating off the earth and blinding me. The coffee in my cup has gone lukewarm and bitter. I can hear Carol behind me now, up and moving about inside with another pot, with breakfast.

I won't wait for her this morning. I will fold these pages in two, slip them inside the sleeve of the envelope addressed to you. Then I will walk past Manuela's down to the end of the alley where the earth dissolves into sand and sinks the last few metres to the water. Along the shore the sea grass will lie piled and stretched having washed in during the night, slashing dark and ugly the soft white sand. Upon the water I will lay this letter, watch the water take it into its hold and suck it under, watch the ink spread across the white face. Your name, Kate, will splinter into many long ribbons, the paper that holds it together becoming heavy and thin and sheer. I will watch it break apart. Then I will sit at the edge where the sand is damp and watch the tide carry you away to a shore where someone else watches back and waits for something to strike out of nothing, as though guided by an unseen hand.

MIA GALLAGHER

Mia Gallagher is the author of two critically acclaimed novels: *Beautiful Pictures of the Lost Homeland* (New Island, 2016), longlisted for the Republic of Consciousness Award, and *HellFire* (Penguin Ireland, 2006), recipient of the *Irish Tatler* Literature Award. Her short fiction has been published widely, winning the START award in 2005 and shortlisted for Hennessy, Fish and Trevor/Bowen Awards.

'All Bones' was previously published in the 2003 Fish Anthology and as part of a limited edition chapbook *You First* (South Tipperary Arts Centre, 2005). Mia is the 2017 Farmleigh Writer-in-Residence and a contributing editor to *The Stinging Fly*. With the assistance of an Arts Council of Ireland bursary, she is currently working on a story collection, due for publication in 2018, and a new novel.

All Bones

Dark. Sweaty. Bass pounding. Bodies heaving. Overhead arched windows, looking out onto black. In the centre of the dance floor Neil knelt down, seeing a thousand stars humming a song of eternity. He was out of his face on acid.

She was in the corner, moving like some crazy disjointed mannequin. Her shaved head glowed sick green in the bad disco lights. She was all bones. The light changed green to blue to red to white, turning her from sea-creature to madonna to devil to skeleton.

The thought made it happen.

Her eyes stared at him, empty black holes. She began to move towards him.

Coming to get you.

She slid her way across, slipping between the other bodies lumbering rhythmic on the floor, so thin that to his tripping eyes she seemed to be melting between them, coating them with a transparent patina of girl.

Now she was in front of him. Stone Age cheekbones, huge eyes, thin thin thin hands, waving seaweed fingers. She danced like a maniac, elbows, knees everywhere. Her rhythm was off, kept catching him by surprise, but slowed down by the acid, he enjoyed the sudden shifts, went with them.

Outside, she mouthed.

He followed her through the ecclesiastical passage-ways of the deconsecrated building. She came and went in the darkness.

Wait, he kept saying. *Wait for me.* Except he was so out of his face he couldn't tell if he said it out loud or not.

She drew him into a room filled with red light and angular mechanical objects, sinks, plastic bottles full of dark liquids. *Alchemy,* he thought. *Far fucking out.* She waved a key in his face and kicked the door shut behind him.

How the — he began to think, then stopped as she placed her mouth on his like a wet soft hand and dug her tongue in.

She was voracious. Her lips were full and moist, soft cushions. They belonged to a fat girl.

Down, down onto the ground.

'Hey, easy,' he said at one point, distracted from his orgasm, from the feeling of it, which he wanted to savour because usually you don't you know, but this time, with the acid he could, because it was so…except she kept fucking bouncing, like a Duracell rabbit on speed.

'Easy.'

She stopped. Shame flooded her face, in the acid bath of his head distorting her into something by Goya.

'Come live with me,' she said. Come fly away.

She lived in a tiny house in the inner city. Red-brick, two-up, two-down. Or, in this case, one-and-a-half-up, two-down. She was very practical about it. That surprised him. He'd expected her to be more demanding.

But no, she explained. Her flatmate had just moved out and she needed somebody to share with because she couldn't afford it on her own. She was a photographer. On the dole, no money, living off favours and other people's darkrooms.

Neil needed a place to stay. His ex had chucked him out, rents had exploded and there was no way he could afford somewhere on his own.

'Okay,' he said, still dubious at the way she'd dug his mobile number out of thin air.

'Don't worry.' She exhaled cigarette smoke from the corner of her mouth. 'I won't bite.'

She was American, Kentucky originally, but years of hustling in New York had eradicated any trace of a Southern accent. She presented herself as being tough as nails, as an old boot, as something that had been left out in the rain for years.

He was given the bad room, the half-room, the one she had to walk through on her way downstairs each morning. She had the front room, the whole one with the big window and the floor space and the ten strong wooden shelves.

She owned nothing. No pots and pans. No plants. No pictures. One day Neil stuck up two posters on the landing wall. When she saw them she turned sour, resentful, as if he'd walked in on her while she was asleep and pissed on her bed.

One afternoon, when he was bored and sick of watching *Jerry Springer* and *Police Stop!* re-runs, he decided to poke around. She was out on an assignment, meeting friends, something intense. All her appointments were loaded with the same intensity.

He stuck his head around the thick black curtain that worked as a door between their rooms. He couldn't get over how empty her space was. No clothes, apart from a functional shop-rail of baggy grey and black workwear and a row of clunky boots. No ornaments, no girlish things. In one corner a tripod and three cameras, arranged like precious heirlooms. In another, a grey filing cabinet. It was as bleak as a prisoner's cell, he thought, somewhere a monk would sleep.

He wondered if he should go in. Why not? It wasn't as if he was going to steal anything.

The shelves were full of hard-backed folders containing slides. Nothing interesting, just her work: landscapes, cityscapes, her own body. She was obsessed with her body. He tried to open the filing cabinet, hoping to find diaries or some other evidence of who she really was, but it was locked. He gave up and was about to leave when he saw a scrap of paper sticking out behind the edge of the cabinet. It must have dropped there but she hadn't bothered picking it up.

He teased it out.

A round-faced all-American teenager, sitting on the back of a red Cadillac, big yellow fields stretching behind her. Endless America. She had apple-pink cheeks and curly brown hair that fell in spirals down to her shoulders. She was a big girl, strong and fit but definitely on the large side. Her arms were freckled, her face glowed.

Later that evening when she came in, moody and on edge because her meeting hadn't gone well, he searched for the farm girl in what she was now. He couldn't find her; she was long gone, reduced to almost nothing.

They fucked again from time to time, mainly when they were pissed, but never in her bed. Instead, the cheap uncomfortable sitting-room sofa, the kitchen table – a clumsy experience that left him with a black eye after he knocked a saucepan off one of the shelves – and his small, single bed. She bounced on him like a demon, urging, all bones. Turned off, he usually came close to losing his hard-on, except then he'd think of something – a gash mag, the model in the Smirnoff Ice ad (undressed, of course), ex-girlfriends, the sweetie from his favourite café – and freed from service to the untenable moment, would come.

She never did. Nor did she pretend to. He wondered about that, but never for too long. It wasn't something they could talk about. One night when they'd been smoking grass, she opened her mouth, frowning, and he thought she was going to say something. But he'd just jizzed, was in a world of his own, pleasant, warm and sated, and not really in the mood for going into all that. She must have read him because, instead of talking, she reached for the grass and rolled up another joint. And that was that. He didn't feel bad about it. He got the feeling it was easier for her not to go there; that way she wouldn't have to dissolve that wall of transparent ice she'd constructed around herself.

She ate nothing. Okay, not quite nothing, but as far as Neil – born and bred on rashers and eggs, beans and chips, hot dinners, chocolate and crisps – was concerned, sweet fuck all. Bowls of steamed fruit first thing in the morning, followed by some mess of cereal you wouldn't give a dog. Salad for lunch. Rice and vegetables, occasionally, at night.

One night when he was jarred he mentioned, jocularly, that she could do with some fattening up. She went still, the fag at her mouth seeming to freeze too, even its smoke hanging, poised, in mid-air.

'Oops,' he said, trying to joke his way out of it. 'Touchy subject.'

She extracted the fag and blew a stream of smoke towards the telly. He noticed that her fingers were shaking. She didn't say anything, just zapped to Channel 4.

The next night he went clubbing and brought another girl home. The sweetie from his favourite café. She was lithe and small and brown, with large breasts that fell into his E-sensitised hands like pieces of heaven. She came loudly, twice.

See? he thought, satisfied, imagining her in the room beside them, awake, listening, crying.

He was afraid to wank in case she'd hear.

She woke religiously, same time every morning. Seven. On the odd day Neil was awake then too, he'd hear her get out of bed. Then it would start. The heavy breathing from behind the black curtain. Ee-aw-ee-aw. He imagined her masturbating, lying on the sanded floor, legs open, pressing that tired fleshless button of hers, willing something to happen. Ee-aw. For twenty minutes, then she'd scoot up and race down to the shower as if frightened he'd get there first.

One night she came in rat-arsed from an opening and forgot the pull the curtain over properly. The next morning he woke, too early, burning with the beginnings of a flu, unable to get back to sleep. From next door he could hear the breathing. Ee-aw. Harsh, fast, slow, fast. He couldn't stand it anymore, lying there, listening, that gap in the curtain calling to him, so he crawled down his bed and peeked through.

She was doing push-ups, naked. Her muscled back shone blue and orange in the early morning streetlamps. Her tiny buttocks clenched together. Her shaven head raised, lowered, raised. Downy hairs lifted up all over her skin. The tendons of her arms stood out like the knobbled bits on an Aran jumper. Her breath was harsh and fast.

Poor bitch, he thought, surprising himself with his pity.

He usually went out on Sundays but that week his parents were down the country, denying him roast dinner and the use of their washing machine. The sweetie from the café had gone back to Barcelona and his mates were all split up: canoeing holiday, business conference and an open-air festival that he couldn't afford.

She was going out.

'There's this old market in the centre,' she explained, as he drank his coffee. 'I want to capture it before they tear it down and turn it into another fucking pub for tourists.'

'Tourists?' said Neil, slyly.

'And fuck you.' She stubbed out her cigarette and, before he could say *Oh but I have* — 'D'you want to come along?'

'Okay,' he said, surprising himself again. 'Why not?'

They headed off around four. Neil helped her carry her cameras. She'd brought all three of them. One standard 35mm, one digital video – a present from back home, she said – and one square brown box Neil didn't recognise. 'Large-format,' she explained. 'Takes incredible pictures, super candid.'

Town was busy in the usual places but the crowds started thinning out as they got closer to the market. Rats deserting a sinking ship, lice fleeing a comb.

'Okay,' she said, 'here.' She set the tripod down.

The building was large, glass-roofed, littered with old pallets and fruit papers. Oranges rolled in corners, bruised and oozing rancid juice. Scraps of tattered cloth dangled from the peak of the roof. Ancient signs, painted with the names of fruit & veg families who'd been there for centuries, hung overhead.

It was cold.

'There was a church here once,' she said. 'Underneath.'

Neil thought of dark ecclesiastical passageways and black arched windows.

'They say people are buried there.'

'People?'

'Yeah.'

She began taking pictures. She was deliberate in her work. She would stand for minutes, looking, looking, smelling almost more than seeing, then move, decisive but not rushing, to the place where she wanted to work, line up her camera, look through the lens, wait again – for ages it seemed to him, afterwards he thought it must have been to get the light right – then click. The click was over so quickly, compared to the waiting.

Jesus, he thought. *If only she could fuck the way she worked.*

It grew darker.

'Shouldn't we go?' he said. 'I mean, the light…'

She shook her head. 'No. This is the best hour. Things come out of the walls at this time of day.'

Left with no choice, he had to keep watching. Look, wait, smell, listen, bend, look, move the camera forward a bit, up a bit. She touched the camera with small gentle movements, as if it was a little child she was training to walk. It responded. They were dancing together, he realised. She and the camera, dancing in the dark.

As he observed her, he became calm. Her stillness leaked into him like pus.

'Why don't we explore?' he asked. The pictures were on the verge of being finished, he could tell that – by the way her head was inclining, perhaps, by a restlessness starting to itch itself into her right foot. He could tell she was about to finish and he didn't want her to. Anything would do, anything to keep things as they were.

'Oh.' She turned, surprised. 'I was about to —'

'Yeah,' he said. 'But, why not – I mean – you never know what we might find.'

'Sure,' she said. Half-smiling. A small puzzled frown on her forehead.

They came across the door in a corner of the market, hidden behind a metal trolley laden with pallets and empty fruit boxes. It was not as he'd imagined it, oak and gothic, but square, dull-grey, sheet metal.

Someone had been there before them. One edge of the door was twisted up and away, jimmied with a knife or chisel. He stuck his fingers into the gap and pulled. The door screamed, metal against metal, and opened a fraction. It was too small a gap for him to get through. He slid in his arm.

'Chancing your arm,' she said. 'Like the Normans.'

'What?'

'That's where the saying comes from. The Normans used to stick their sword arms through this eentsy hole in the door so they could, you know, break through.'

'Yeah?' he said. He couldn't budge it.

'Hey, let me.'

'You won't,' he said, looking at the gap between the edge of the door and the wall.

'Trust me.'

She turned herself sideways and edged her knee into the impossible space.

Her shoulder disappeared, then her hip. Half of her body was on the other side of the door. She made a small, sighing sound and manoeuvred her other hip through.

'Ugh. Tight.'

'Yeah,' he said, feeling darkness creep up behind him.

'Okay! Head.'

She squeezed her head backwards through the gap. It made him nauseous, thinking of the fragile bones in her skull, weakened by stewed fruit and too many push-ups, turn liquid under the pressure of metal and stone.

The tendons on her neck stood out, parallel lines, vulnerable. He wanted to touch them, stroke them as you would a baby's face. She melted into nothing.

'Okay.' From the other side, her voice was echoing and dark. 'I'm gonna push.'

You can't, he thought. Then he remembered her daily grind of push-ups, the muscles on her body standing up like knitted blackberry stitch.

She pushed. The door screamed and shuddered.

Come on, come on, he thought, not wanting to be stuck in the darkening empty market like some forlorn ghost. The door screamed again.

'Grab it!' Her voice was muffled.

He seized the edge of the door and pulled. From the other side he felt the force of her body push; so much force for such a small body.

'Okay!' he called. 'Coming through!'

The pencil beam of her Maglite shone on crumbling stone walls, moss, blackened rock, a few half-broken steps.

'Be prepared,' said Neil, indicating the light.

She ignored him.

At the bottom of the stairs was a second door. Much more like it. Panelled wood with iron clasps, set into a Gothic arch. It had been pulled well off its hinges and swung open without a bother.

Inside, it was cold and damp, the floor slippery. Fungus glowed in the corners. The Maglite flickered on ruined benches, pieces of rotten wood, pews missing backrests and feet, crumbling arched recesses where holy pictures had once stood. At the top, what must have been the altar – a raised bank of stone speckled with lichen, covered with beer cans and cigarettes.

Neil laughed. 'Jesus. I thought it was just a story.'

'Sshh,' she said, finger on her lips

Fucksake, he thought. *It's not a museum.*

At the back of the altar was a raised wooden casket. One of the doors hung loose on its hinge, the other was fastened tight. She walked up to it.

'Hey,' he said, wanting to warn her but not sure why.

She ignored him and, using one finger, swung the closed half-door open.

'Oh fuck!' She stepped back. Her torch clattered onto the ground, sending shadows racing over the walls. The Maglite snapped off. They were in blackness.

'Oh Jesus!' She began to heave dry retches.

'Jule?' said Neil, on instinct calling her name, the way you'd call a hurt dog.

She started crying.

'It's okay,' said Neil. 'It's okay.' He couldn't see where she was but moved towards the sound of her retching, her sobbing.

'It's okay. I'm here.' His outstretched hands came in contact with warmth, cheekbones, wet face.

He closed his arms around her. She crumpled into him, still sobbing.

'Okay,' he said. 'Ssshh.'

He kissed her forehead. She pressed into him, sniffling. His hands stroked her goose-pimpled arms, the hairs that stood up on end. Behind her, as his eyes adjusted to the darkness, he saw something white gleam against the blackness of the altar.

'Easy,' he said. This time she listened.

'They were bones,' she told him as they walked home hand in hand through Dublin's deepening blue evening. 'Children's bones. I could see their little faces and legs and —'

'It's okay,' he said and squeezed her hand. She squeezed back, fingers thin thin thin like river reeds, autumn twigs.

JAMES MARTYN JOYCE

James Martyn Joyce is from Galway. His poetry collection, *Shedding Skin*, was published in 2010 and his short story collection, *What's Not Said*, was published in 2012. He edited a collection of short stories, *Noir by Noir West*, in 2014. His new collection of poetry, *Furey*, will be published by Doire Press in spring 2018.

The Man Who Ran

Once, I worked with a guy who was a born-again robber. I had just finished college and there weren't many options flying around, so I took a job in a small bakery. There were eight of us between bakers and helpers and drivers. There were daytime people upstairs in the office, as well, but we never saw them.

All the workers said the place was haunted. It was in one of the oldest parts of town, with bones just below the cobbles if you dug, and sometimes the bones rattled and peeked through if you weren't careful.

I figured they were trying to scare me, the new fella, giving me the 'wooo, wooo' treatment. But from time to time I heard strange noises and things falling in the yard where they kept the vans. No one would go out there in the dark for any reason. But that was where we kept the yeast, so we made sure to have a good supply inside and soaking before darkness fell. The boss man, whom we never saw, insisted that the yeast supply be kept under lock and key or we'd all be selling it to the hooch makers in the mountains. That was how he saw it anyway.

Truth was, we were bakers; we worked in the dark. In winter, we'd plan ahead and bring a supply of yeast inside in the morning and hide it behind the sink. It was getting bright by then and we'd scoot across the yard, usually two of us, slip the lock on the yeast store and be back inside before the cobbles rattled. There was a way around everything.

It was the same with stealing bread. We all did it. The younger baker, who started way before us in the evenings, had about nineteen brothers and sisters, both married and unmarried. At the end of his shift, he would load a shopping bag with large loaves and a second bag with smaller ones to distribute amongst his many siblings on his midnight meander home.

The younger baker told us to steal all our bread on his shift because the senior man, who started at midnight, and who had a lisp, spat openly into the deep sink. He also did what we called 'suck-backs': great reversals of snot and mucus which he would launch in the general direction of the sink where the yeast sat percolating in large, once-white buckets. We could never be sure of his accuracy and sometimes we wouldn't be positioned to see the comets land. This worried us. So we stole our bread early and wrapped it in whatever we could find to keep it fresh.

When Jody came to work with us he made an impression early on. He told us first that it was with a -y, his name that is, and not to forget it. In his last job, before he left Dublin, he'd almost killed some guy who reckoned it was a girl's name and said so. They had a 'straightener' out behind the cold stores and the other guy almost didn't live to regret it.

I could well believe it. Jody wasn't very big, but what there was of him was solid, pure muscle and bone, with an air off him which made you think, 'Jody with a -*y* is fine by me.' We got on well from the start.

He would look at you by turning his whole upper body, like he was giving you his full attention. When we became close he told me it was because he'd been hit in the head with a paving slab during a riot in Mountjoy prison where he'd served three years. It had damaged his neck and he had tunnel vision as well. He never said what he served the three years for, just curled his fist, turned his whole upper torso towards me, focused and said, 'Ya know yerself?' That explained it.

He'd run away to Galway to make a fresh start, so he said. There were men looking for him on the east coast – and possibly on the north coast too. He wouldn't be going back. But he hadn't run alone. He had a wife with him.

I met them on Shop Street one Saturday, a week or two after he started, and he introduced me to Cherine. A 'skinny leggings' sort of girl, thin but interesting, she was younger than Jody and classy. But it was her clavicles I noticed first. They just looked enticing, translucent almost, like they were leading somewhere. Jody liked them too, he kissed them a lot while we were chatting, and I kept noticing.

She had black bangs as well. I didn't even know what they were called, at first, but she caught me looking.

'Do you like my bangs, Jimmy?' She inclined her head, and her hair closed around her face like mini theatre curtains until only her eyes were visible. That was more than enough for Jody, and he kissed her clavicles again.

Cherine wasn't her real name, but he didn't tell me that at the time. It was her running name, the name she chose when they ran away together. He told me the story the following Monday night while we were greasing tins when I said I thought his wife was nice.

'*The* wife, Jimmy,' he emphasised. 'The wife.'

'Yes,' I agreed. 'Your wife.'

'She's not my wife, Jimmy. She's another guy's wife' was how he broke the news. 'We worked together in the last place. She was in the office. We've run away because I love her so much. And she treasures that.'

'You're not married then?'

'We are. The both of us, just not to each other. That's why I call her "the wife".'

That was the week after the senior baker, with his lisp and his flying mucus, had tried to make sure that Jody found out about the haunted yard and used all of us as collaborating jokesters. None of us liked the senior baker, and not just because of his hygiene problems, but we were afraid of him and played along. He'd stand at the kneading table and bellow:

'Pwull the twop one.' And we'd have to grab the long irons, slip the catches on the plate-oven, inhale the blast and slide the baked breads out, the waves of heat sweating us. We reckoned he timed the 'pulls' to make us work extra hard because you'd only have the first batch of loaves on the scorched boards when he'd smile and call: 'Now, pwull the bwottom one.' And we'd have to repeat the whole procedure, the sweat soaking us even more, the smell of baked bread leaching into our wet skins.

Well, that night we'd just pulled both ovens when the senior baker told Jody to fetch two packs of yeast from the store across the yard and took the key from his pocket. He handed the key to Jody along with a twenty-cent coin and said: 'Here's a penny for yourself.' This was a ploy he used with anyone who got tested for the yeast run. It made the runner feel humiliated, small, and less than manly. Then he laughed and went back to his rolls of dough.

Well, Jody took the key and the coin and crossed the yard. If he batted an eyelid none of us saw it and he marched back with two packs of yeast and the key and left them on the baker's worktop. Then he produced a fair-sized hammer from his back pocket and what looked like a three-inch nail and hammered the twenty-cent coin to the wooden workbench.

'Now.' He smiled. 'There's yer penny. I'd be upset if you lost it.' And he rested the hammer, very lightly, on the senior baker's chest. 'You won't lose it now, will you?' I don't know which looked paler right then, the baker's face or the floury worktop.

Then Jody came over to where we were greasing tins and winked at me as he took the rag, dug it into the tub of yellow fat and began smearing the tins with the baker still looking after him. I never found out where he got the hammer, or the nail, but the baker never sent another new boy out for yeast and humiliation while I was there.

It was the young baker's shift, and we were all making our arrangements. My needs were slim; I usually took a small loaf and a French stick. I'd met a girl that I liked a few months before and we'd moved in together. She liked the softness of the white flesh she pulled from the centre of the French stick and smothered it in butter.

'Are you taking any bread?'

'No.' Jody watched as I slipped the stick into the sleeve of my anorak, just in case the boss man came in early and ambushed us on the way out.

'No? Would Cherine not fancy a French stick?' He knew I was chancing it, but he just smiled.

'I don't steal anymore since I met her. She doesn't like it; she says that someone is always at a loss. She thinks it leaves a gap in the universe if you steal, or something like that. Yeah, the last thing I stole was two trout.'

'Two trout?'

'Yeah, two frozen trout. I had one down each pocket of my jeans and I gave her a lift home from work in the van.'

'And?'

'We weren't living together then, but we used to go down to the seafront at Clontarf for a…you know yerself?' and he smiled. 'Well when she felt the stiff coldness in my jeans she almost jumped out the van window.'

'Jayzzz?' I tried not to smile. He turned his whole torso towards me.

'*Suppose you have a crash?* That was what she said. And then I saw it, me rushed to hospital, unconscious, dead maybe, with a frozen trout in each trouser pocket? Can you see it?' I could. Unfortunately. '*You'd be in all the tabloids*, she said. *They'd end up calling you a fishophile, or something.*'

So he didn't steal bread, or anything else, which is why I was so surprised when he got involved in the robbery. I didn't notice until afterwards but that last week he took to coming in every evening and asking me geography questions. Not the mountains or rivers sort. No, but he'd say: 'Jimmy? If you walk down Shop Street and over O'Brien's Bridge and go left, what street are you on?'

'Dominick Street, Jody.'

'Dominick Street? Right. And, if you go right at the end of that street and keep slightly right again, where's that?'

'Then, you're on Henry Street.'

'And if you go straight on to the traffic lights at the end there?'

'That's Cooke's Corner.'

I only realised afterwards that he was learning the town, taking it in, street by street, back lane and pathway, shortcut and skip-out, until he had it all mapped in his mind and he could outrun anyone.

The day it happened he'd worked the night shift as usual. He arrived, he worked, he eyeballed the senior baker and he stole no bread. When I was leaving with a French stick down each sleeve of my anorak (me and the bread girl were a real item now; she was eating more and putting on weight; I liked it), he was standing at the long wooden workbench, absentmindedly stroking the twenty-cent coin, smoothing his finger around the edge, running his thumb across the shiny bronzed centre, snagging his nail on the nail head.

'Penny for your thoughts?' I couldn't resist it.

'Jimmy?' He turned full on to face me. 'Cherine's going to leave.'

'Has she said? Back to Dublin?'

'No, but I can just feel it. She'll try London, she said it before. Her fella would kill her if she went home now.'

'And yourself?' I asked. He focused somewhere around my Adam's apple.

'I have one shot left. Maybe I'll hold on to her. I'll know today.' Then he fumbled a bit of paper and handed it to me. 'This is where we live. It's up along the canal, before Cooke's Corner. If I'm not at work tomorrow, will you put her on the GoBus to the airport?'

'Sure, Jody. Sure.' I figured he was being dramatic but I'd do it anyway. I was about to look at the address but the senior baker came in, all wind and piss as usual, so I just pocketed it and headed for home. The bread girl would be waiting.

Well, by the time we'd started back to work that same evening, it was all over the news. Three men wearing balaclavas had tried to rob a local bakery owner as he was about to lodge the week's takings at a bank on Eyre Square. That wasn't the worst of it. The leader, or apparent leader, had struggled with the bakery owner and the gun had gone off, hitting a second robber in the chest, killing him instantly. Then the leader had shot the bakery owner, wounding him, and was about to shoot him again when the third robber, who moved with a peculiar upright gait, had knocked the gunman unconscious, grabbed the money bag and ran.

One elderly man who'd witnessed the whole thing said that the robber had run like Michael Johnson, the winner at some Olympics or other. This had set everyone Googling on their phones and we all came up with the same image. Witnesses said he ran down Shop Street, pumping his arms, left onto Dominick Street, right on to Henry Street and straight through Cooke's Corner.

I followed the trail in my head. Everyone had seen him, the funny, upright gait, the lean-back, hammer-arm style. He was so noticeable they remembered him even after he'd discarded the balaclava.

I knew it was Jody, I knew he was running for Cherine but the funny thing was he just kept on going. He sprinted straight through Cooke's Corner and up Shantalla Road where he ran headlong into a police car speeding to the scene of the robbery after sorting out a domestic incident over on the Westside. Jody ran straight into them, almost crossed the bonnet,

and the three policemen – well, two men and a woman
– nabbed him, no bother.

We were all over it at work, and every driver
who came back from the day's deliveries added to
the story. The big boss man – for it was indeed our
beloved boss who had been shot – was dead, dying on
the operating table undergoing a six-hour operation,
travelling home in a taxi, or paralysed from the waist
down, depending on which version you believed. But
they all agreed that Jody was in custody and would
be tried for attempted murder, even if he'd saved the
boss's life by kicking the leader senseless before he
could shoot him a second time.

I caught the early news the next morning when I
got home. The bread girl was sleeping and I knew
I had to shower before I could crawl into bed beside
her. She was pregnant and the smell of the yellow
grease could really set her off. I sat on the arm of the
old sofa and followed the details of the story as they
unfolded.

The police were still looking for the money and
the home address of the robber who'd been arrested
on Shantalla Road. There was a shot of Jody with a
coat over his head being led into the police station
on Mill Street. I recognised the stiff way he walked
and the sweatshirt he was wearing. I drew the small
fold of paper from my pocket and read the address. I
knew then that he'd made a short detour before racing
through Cooke's Corner and I figured I knew where
the money was.

I showered and changed into my street clothes, took my bicycle from the front room and headed for the canal. I didn't expect Cherine to be waiting. I thought she'd be long gone, but when I rang the doorbell on the garage flat I saw the curtains twitch and she opened the door.

It was an old-style money bag, all crinkled leather and worn, with a brass lock. She'd hacked through the base where the leather was thinnest. The money lay in dirty rolls on the small table. We walked from there to the bus station, me wheeling the bike and she towing her suitcase and we didn't really speak. We even passed the scene of the crime, rubbernecking with the best of them, the place thick with police.

She booked on, no bother, and then she turned, stood close to me and kinda pulled at the third button down on my shirt.

'I didn't want him to do it, Jimmy. I told him we'd be fine.' The tears shone in her eyes.

'He told me you were threatening to leave, that he had only one shot left.' I knew I was angry.

'We had a terrible row about a week back, said awful things, both of us. He felt he wasn't giving me enough. But I'd never have left him, never.' She was crying now.

Well, who knows with two people? Not me anyway. I barely knew myself and the pregnant bread girl back in bed in Newcastle. So I looked at her almost translucent clavicles and kissed her forehead lightly and she went and sat halfway down the bus. She leant her face forward until her bangs covered her face and

I knew she was still crying. I took my bike and cycled out to Newcastle. I thought of all that money just sitting there on the table near Cooke's Corner as I slipped into bed and cuddled the bread girl's dainty bump. She mumbled something nice with 'love' in it, pushed her bum into me, and we slept.

ROSALEEN McDONAGH

Rosaleen McDonagh is a Traveller woman with a disability. She worked in Pavee Point Traveller and Roma Centre for ten years, where she jointly managed the Violence Against Women programme. McDonagh's work includes *The Baby Doll Project, Stuck, She's Not Mine*, and *Rings. Rings* was performed at VAS in Washington in June 2010. McDonagh was shortlisted for the PJ O' Connor Radio Play Awards 2010. While in the United States with Fishamble, Colum McCann, Booker Prize winner, gave her the rights to adapt his 2007 novel, *Zoli*, for stage. In March 2012, *Beat Him Like a Badger* was commissioned by Fishamble to be part of the Tiny Plays for Ireland series. Rosaleen has a Bachelor of Arts in Biblical and Theological Studies, an M.Phil in Ethnic and Racial Studies and an M.Phil in Creative Writing, all from Trinity College Dublin. She is currently a PhD candidate at Northumbria University. *Mainstream* was produced by Project Arts Centre and directed by Jim Culleton in 2016. Rosaleen has served two terms on the NWCI and is an active board member. She was elected to Aosdána in March 2017 and is a board member of Project Arts Centre.

Mangled

8th of March 2017: International Women's Day, Dublin. Temperatures are high for mid-spring. Quickly scanning the crowd, Bella speculates that there could be at least twenty thousand people on the street. Families of various compositions are in the majority. Children bemused by the spectacle. The throng of people are full of idealism. The noise! Whistles being blown. Samba drums being banged to a multitude of beats. The crowd is high on adrenaline. Conversations and murmurs reverberate. Selfies are taken from side angles. Despite the organisers' efforts to create a political demonstration, the march has a more festival feel to it. Bella is trying to lose herself in the crowd.

Watching the march pass from a footpath, she is squeezed into a horde of people leaning over her wheelchair, their gentle pushing and shoving. Bodies are touching. Their proximity feels dangerous. Apologies are given, with equal amounts of head patting. Handbags being swung unintentionally into her face add to the carnival atmosphere. Panic comes in waves. The straw is crushed and bent in the bottom of the bag. Holding the water bottle up to her mouth is becoming exhausting. The mayhem is distressing. She has deliberately avoided public spaces for the last fifteen or twenty years. Crowds feel too much. For a brief second she whispers: *what am I doing here?*

At the top of the march there is a group of deaf and disabled women with CONSENT written across their t-shirts. The chanting and the sweat of euphoria gather momentum. Women disperse from their caucus and mingle with intention and precision. Rainbow flags are in full swing. Catchphrases derived from feminist mantras illustrate how the language of human rights has expanded through the decades.

The shrill sound of a whistle makes Bella jump. Applause bursts and ripples through the crowd. People start moving from The Garden of Remembrance towards O'Connell Street. Stewards try in vain to corral people into a safe way of marching. Megaphones muffle voices and render them incoherent. Chants are repeated loudly and then peter off. There are quieter moments where reflection and far away thoughts pass over people's faces. There is a sigh of exasperating impatience and the sorrow is infectious. Bella has learned that reading women's faces brings open-ended conjecture.

A woman in her early twenties with pink symmetrical hair leads the group. Earlier, people were queuing to be photographed with her. She stops the sporty wheelchair directly where Bella is positioned. All movement has slowed down. The crowd further back don't understand what the commotion is.

Pink Hair indicates that there is room next to her on the street. The crowds either side of Bella part, ushering her to join the group. In her vintage wheelchair Bella puts her head down, hoping all this will stop. Fear and nervousness, familiar feelings, make her want to get lost on a different street. Pink Hair is bold and insistent. Flashing cameras: the attention is on Bella and the young woman. The media are opportunistic; Bella watches Pink Hair posturing for the cameras and wonders if the moment was orchestrated.

Moving forward, Bella finds herself in the group between wheelchair users and Traveller women. The banner is put in front of her. It says: MY BODY, MY CHOICE. There are a few women in hijabs and jeans, pushing prams. One of the Traveller women is carrying a megaphone. The chant is 'diversity and equality.'

You're going to need this. Water isn't strong enough. Pink Hair offers Bella a swig from her hip flask. She is pouty and mouthy. *You will be smothered in that crowd.*

The young woman warns Bella not to say a word to the journalists. Bella leans in and whispers: *don't tell your grandmother how to suck eggs.*

Pink Hair starts ranting: *autonomy, freedom and control over our bodies.* Holding the crowd's attention she bellows: *The history of eugenics – institutionalisation segregated education the right to bodily integrity the continuous infantilisation of Disabled lives.* The crowd is enthralled. Another woman in the group shouts: *take that fucking megaphone off her.* Everybody close by bursts into laughter. Bella hands back the hip flask. Pink Hair takes a long drink. Bella falls into step with the Traveller women. Her mind wanders back thirty years.

8th March 1987: turbulence between Birmingham and Dublin.

The pilot announces that they will be another forty minutes in the air. It is a night flight home. Her nausea, cigarette smoke, the low hum of the cabin, artificial lighting: the combination makes Bella feels weak. The hemorrhaging is sporadic. Her body is tired and sore. Coming back to Dublin feels more traumatic than leaving.

The staff in the clinic were professional. The receptionist made a reference to Bella's soft Irish lilt. The remark hung in the air as if it had been said to thousands of others. There were no comments, questions or judgments. They told her to take two Nurofen and then go to bed. But that was a luxury for another day.

A woman on the plane walks past several times on her way to the toilet. Anonymity is something Bella doesn't have. Their eyes lock in recognition. The silence and guilt was the glue that held the gaze. Bella remembered thinking how women instinctively police each other. The compromise is always about secrecy and silence.

As the flight attendant handed Bella a straw, the flashbacks grew more vivid. *They never ask if I need a straw*, he said. She was naive; she was passive. *That's what your family have done to you*, he said. *Having people*

stare and look — it's hurtful. Loving you is challenging.
Regardless of the context he would make a scene.
Bella didn't care. Sitting on the plane wiping tears
away, she wondered how the hell she got into this
mess. Rows over straws?

Many years after the break-up with Joe, Bella
started therapy. Her therapist helped her realise how
destructive their relationship had been. Joe sometimes
forced himself. It didn't feel like violence. His need for
sex was natural. Everything he wanted to do to her
body she let him. Different positions that hurt. He
encouraged her to focus on the pleasure rather than
the pain. Frequently during the night she would wake
up to find Joe on top of her. For years he never seemed
to hear her saying the word no. Her parents often
questioned why she, who had always been gregarious
and loud, had learned to speak in whispers. Bella told
the therapist that she wasn't a victim. She wasn't one
of those women. The therapist nodded, handing her
tissues. *Nobody is one of those women,* she said.

Her progressive condition would be too easy to
blame. The truth of the matter was wrong time,
wrong place, and wrong man. The vista was bigger.
More nuanced. Reasons, rationales and reflections
couldn't be reduced to one significant motivation.
People find themselves in tight corners.

They talked about her attraction to Joe. Self-assured
and charismatic, his age had made him interesting. He
had a swagger. Bella could not believe that a man like
Joe would be interested in a woman like her. The law
degree that he had never finished was always a source

of rage. He ended up doing bar work. He thought this was beneath him. During Bella's final year in college he would question why she was putting all this pressure on herself. What was she trying to prove? *You don't owe your family anything.*

Bella never told Joe about the brief flings she had before meeting him. Joe assumed that she was a virgin. Like always, Bella never corrected or contradicted his view. She was passive and pretty. This is what he told her, this is what she was. He frightened her into this performance. Soon after they started sleeping together, he began referring to her placidness as the reason she was so uptight and unadventurous. He said she lacked passion and ingenuity. She was afraid to trust or try different ways of having sex. He had to be in charge, always having to take the lead. He really didn't want to be that kind of man but Bella left him no option.

Don't let him take over the place. Her mother's words rang in her ear.

When Joe moved into her apartment the rest of the world thought that they were a great couple. Joe pointed out that all women had issues that stopped them liking their bodies. He explained that some women, like her, were doubly disadvantaged. Bella had thought this was profound and insightful. She had never heard a man say such a thing before. He oozed with sensitivity and knowledge. He liked women to be women and not get caught up with labels. Once, at a party, she heard him describe himself as a feminist to another man. He also said: *it's the best line you can use.*

The body issue was the obvious button to press. He began suggesting a healthier diet. Soon, she realised that he was monitoring what, when and how much she ate.

Whenever Bella received invites to family occasions, Joe's temper would flare up. He had a surprise planned for then, he said. He would withdraw, not speak for a few days. She would spend most of her energy trying to placate him. She never found out what any of the surprises were, and never got to be part of the family celebrations.

Your mother calling over to the apartment when I'm out is intrusive. She doesn't poke her nose in with your other siblings, because they won't let her.

Joe was subtle. One moment he would be warm, cuddly and funny, the next he'd tell her how stupid and slow she really was. In the same breath, he went to great lengths to explain her stupidity had nothing to do with her impairment, it was just the type of woman she was. College education had done nothing for her, whereas the university of life had made him a more insightful man.

He alienated her from her family and friends. Then he encouraged her not to use her electric wheelchair. He preferred her in her manual wheelchair. It was easier for him to manage. He insisted that he liked pushing her. It made her look less disabled, he said. Her power chair was big and clunky, but she loved it.

He had read about this type of thing. The hormones affected women's bodies and minds in all sorts of negative ways. *The pill makes you confused and emotional.* It made it harder for him to support her. Contraception should not be a woman's responsibility. Being careful was his thing. They had unprotected sex because condoms were too small; they spoiled the moment.

Bella knew, like all women know, a change in her body was happening. This change could only be temporary. Her body became a battlefield. Doing the test in the apartment was not possible. He was always there. As well as checking her diary and her handbag, he would also check bins. Bella's only chance was in college.

She repeated the test five days in a row. Her heart stopped each time it turned blue. She woke up feeling sick. The smell of food or detergents would bring it on. Joe had said she was stressed and that working so hard for her exams was at odds with the reality of her disability. Bella was eight weeks pregnant.

Thirty years ago Bella did not know any other disabled women. She imagined they were all locked up in institutions. Joe often wondered aloud, at times he felt he needed a break from the relationship, how she would manage.

It felt like a fable was playing out in her life. During those weeks she had seen three wheelchair users with neat bumps. She guessed that they were four months, seven months, and the last one, probably five months gone. The moment when the stick turned blue, it was the faces of those wheelchair users with their swollen bellies that stared back at her.

The Well Woman Centre. Access – entry and exit and the palaver in between – it would all be too complicated. Birmingham, England. There was a phone number hidden underneath a pile of papers on a notice board. Each woman who found it copied it to a new scrap of paper and re-hid it for another distraught female. Her mam had opened Credit Union accounts for all of her daughters. She called it running away money. Bella had managed to stay away from it until now. The plotting and planning was stressful. The phone calls were difficult, but she managed without having to tell anyone or ask for help.

The tube sucked everything out. Her womb went into contraction. Anaesthetic was offered, with the warning that it would leave her drowsy. Lying on the table. Looking up at the ceiling, its bright lights, crying, desperately wanting her mother. The practice must be done differently now. A tablet. But new technology doesn't change old crises.

It was from a payphone at Birmingham airport that she rang her mam. The conversation was brief. Coming back to Dublin on the same day was not ideal, but if she had waited a night, Joe would have reported her missing.

The airport staff must have been informed because they hurried her through. Joe had been pestering her parents with phone calls every hour. Her parents brought her to the car. Her last memory of Joe was at the airport arrivals screaming, *Bella you are a murderer!*

The crowd begins to fall away. Bella is jaded. She's heading for home. This will be her last march. Altruists and pontificators seem to roll into one big female monologue. Intergenerational conversations are being played out. The space between different women has become smaller. The gauntlet is held by a new generation.

On the opposite side of the road, she sees a man instructing a smaller, less organised group. They are carrying religious pictures. From the edge of the foothpath, Bella can't make out what is written on their placards. Removing her sunglasses, squinting, she sees there is something about disability. The crowd behind her, the crowd in front of her, she, like many other women, are caught in a polarised position. *In supporting women's rights there is also a need to advocate for people with disabilities.* Pink Hair had articulated it earlier.

The Traveller women are still walking together. A woman who walked beside her during the march runs back and gives her a hug. There was a private moment between them. She was talking quietly about her faith, discreetly pulling a medal from under her scarf. Bella showed her the bracelet on her wrist. Saint Christopher. *The patron saint of Travellers,* she giggled. Bella covered her bangle. Pink Hair is in conversation with a handsome man. He's carrying a girl child in a papoose.

She calls Bella back.

Bella ignores the shout.

PAT MCCABE

Pat McCabe was born in Clones, Co. Monaghan, Ireland in 1955.

He has had many novels published including *The Dead School* and *The Butcher Boy*.

His movies include *The Butcher Boy* and *Breakfast on Pluto*, both directed by Neil Jordan.

He is currently performing his 'Analogue Monologue' here and there about the place.

He is married, with two grown-up children, to the artist Margot Quinn, and is a member of Aosdána.

'The Red Menace' an excerpt from *The Big Yaroo*

It's true what they say, at least as far as I'm concerned – that you simply can't open a paper these days but it's all this stuff about Donald Trump and Vladimir Putin, and whether or not there was spying going on during the time when he was running for the elections.

But you can read all you like – go through all the papers until you are practically blue in the face, just so long as you know that by the time you're finished you won't be any the wiser.

As to whether or not he is guilty, I mean. Because one thing they're good at in Russia is covering their tracks.

And the principal main reason for that is that Vladimir Putin used to work for the Stasi in the old days – so there wouldn't be much he wouldn't know about how to go about that – covert operations and everything that goes along with it.

Did you know that he sometimes wrestles bears?

No, he is one client who I most certainly would not be in any hurry to tangle with.

For a long time, I knew absolutely nothing about Russians – even when the whole place was alive with talk about them and what they'd been up to in Cuba at the time. During them good old times of the Lucky Lumps and all the rest when even people who wouldn't even have read a paper or knew where Newtown was never mind St. Petersburg would be taking out their prayer books and pulling you in off the side of the road before announcing:

– Well, that's it now, all we can do is put our trust in the Man above! For come next week we'll all be walking around in a town that's nothing more than a pile of ash!

Before heading off up to the chapel to fire themselves down in front of Our Lady and in the process acquire themselves a substantial heap of what always used to be called back in them times 'plenary indulgences.'

Not that any of that's relevant now seeing as all of that type of thing has long since been done away with, and you can do whatever you like and put it on You Tube and no-one will so much as give one royal fuck.

But there was none of that when I was young – or Rihanna torturing models either. Because what was most important back then was doing your best to get into heaven. And when JFK made his state-of-the-nation appearance on the telly telling everyone that within a matter of weeks we would all of us be chewing dust in our mouths, it was all you ever heard about – prayers and making your final peace with God.

But whose fault was it? That was the other fifty-million dollar question.

Well, regarding that puzzler, it soon emerged that there was very little doubt in absolutely anyone's mind. Because every time you picked up a copy of the *Daily Express* or the *Irish Press*, what did you see on the front of it only perhaps the most fiercest-looking Russian of the whole lot when you get down to it – and that's not Putin or Joseph Stalin or any of the rest of them that you might care to mention – but Nikita Khruschev, if you ever heard tell of him. Who was capable of doing pretty much anything if he took the notion – and if you doubted that then all you had to do was ask, pop up to the parochial house and inquire a bit off Fr. Dan Mc Larnon – who wasn't, at that time, long back from Communist China.

– O don't be talking to me now!

You'd hear him muttering to himself as he came out of the shop. Before hurrying on about his business as if even the very thought of having to think about people, like never mind give you information about them and answer questions, as if that was enough to finish the poor man off.

But one person who had no intention of having that happen to him was Wattlesticks Kiernan who lived in Railway Terrace and if he was alive nowadays would be like one of these fellows that you see who knows practically everything there is to know about eBay or phones or laptops or whatever the fuck.

Because anytime you stopped him he'd start rubbing his hands and tell you that there needn't be anybody worrying their head about Kiernan, for he had everything looked after for 'the time', as he termed it. And which transpired to be the week of the impending nuclear holocaust, when Nikita Khruschev was going to do what he had been threatening to do for close now on six weeks or so. And that was why Wattlesticks announced that he was going to accord us the privilege of a special private tour – of his very own, purpose-built nuclear bunker, which he had only just completed constructing at the bottom of his garden.

And when I tell you that it really was a most impressive structure, you needn't be surprised, because that old Wattles – he wasn't by trade just a builder, as he kept telling us – but a master one. He must have been prattling on for the best part of an hour as me and the rest of the gang just stood there, yawning as much as listening. But, all the same, there could be no denying that it would be a long time before anyone came close to putting together a shelter that would rival it, whether in our little town or the USA or anywhere else.

And which Wattletsicks himself knew only too well. As he rubbed his hands and snorted, with a derisory toss of his head:

– Let Khruschev the baldy fucker come and do his worst – see if I care. Yes, let him do his damnedest to try and do damage to Wattles and all his kin. Look, me son, take a gander over here! Do you see what I've put in? Look over here yonder – a bed that comes folding out from the wall and about as much tinned food as would do any family for fifteen weeks, just in case this Cold War turns hot. And I have all the coal and fuel that we need – and, as well as that, me poor auld father that hasn't been well – he will have his own private quarters. Look here at these walls – six fucking inches of solid massed concrete. So youse would do well to listen when Wattlesticks here decides to give you a piece of advice. And here's some more, me son – that is – them Slavic no-goods would do well to think twice-about coming around this town or anywhere near it. Because Wattles and his friends are more than able for them, and anything they might see fit to throw at us, cataclysm-wise. No, we are far too cute to be caught napping by the likes of them anymore, I'm afraid! So what do youse think of me setup then, lads? Good show?

We assured him that there could be no denying it, which was true. That when it came to the construction of nuclear fallout shelters, Wattlesticks Kiernan was out on his own.

– Whether in this town or anywhere else, we repeated, mimicking his own very words.

We finally set about making our way home – still full of praise for the self-educated mechanic and master-builder's extraordinary workmanship.

Not that it made a whole pile of difference, as everyone of course knows now – considering that neither Khruschev nor Brezhnev or any other fucking 'Slavic no-good' saw fit to bother their backside coming near the place at all – or indeed set off any missiles worth talking about.

Whether in Cuba or anywhere else.

But that doesn't mean you can still talk to me about Russians – for it was them who blinded me, or as good as.

And left me going around the place, like the boys used to say before they left for Portrane, 'like Stevie Wonder.'

Sometimes, when you look back – you can feel so stupid!

Because I can still feel the wallop that they gave me – to this very day I can actually still feel it.

Although I know that most of it was really my own fault – I should never have confronted them that night the way I did. But, like all these things, it's easy to say that now.

I'm not blind entirely – I can still see some things. But what I can make out is always edged in shadow.

Which is why, of course, understandably, that that old Ronners is death on me getting up on bicycles. For who knows where it'll end, like he says.

If you didn't know better you'd swear I made it up – like one of these tall tales you might see in the *National Enquirer.*

I can still see the trapdoor opening that night – and then their big buzzcut breezeblock heads and then the blow and, after that – the crunch!

Boy do them Russian bears pack a wallop! One thump from them, never mind a hail of boots, and it doesn't take long before your optic nerve axons are irreparably damaged, I can tell you.

I miss, though, the world, and the way it used to be – and all the things that used to be in it.

It serves me right, though. And I've often thought: was that my punishment? For having gotten my minders in such terrible trouble, after running away like I did. Because, obviously, they were going to lose their jobs.

Och, poor wee Jake Lafferty & The Fatman Mc Elhinney – them puir wee Donegal lambs, gae their walkin' papers!

It's hard to believe it's nearly sixteen years.

I still get headaches whenever I think about it. All I can remember is:

– Where did he come out of? – In Russian, of course!

And then them battering away at me for what must have been half an hour. And then the police have the gall to ask me did I hurt them? They must have been kicking, as I say, for over half an hour. And would probably still be doing it yet, if I hadn't been fortunate enough to find the machete.

For all I know, they would probably have finished me off.

But, I suppose, like the Master is always saying: briseann an dúchas trí shúile an chait!

Which means, in case you don't know: the nature of the cat will always break through.

And I suppose, to be fair about it, if I had happened to be brought up in Siberia that maybe I'd have thought nothing of doing the very same, kicking the shit out of some strange intruder. Which, of course, is how they would have seen me.

Understandably.

Because, after all, I had appeared right out of nowhere.

And I admit it.

Accept that fair and square.

But, I mean, the fuck – did they have to leave me without a peeper in my bonce?

I mean – for fuck's sake, lads!

Still, there's no use in crying over spilt milk, for what's done is done – and, like everything else, after a while you tend to pretty much get used to it. And they had arranged for me to have a guide dog for a while – a lovely sleek blonde lad who went by the name of Colonel Bruno.

But – you're not going to believe this! – one day I whistled as always – but Bruno didn't come.

With it turning out later that he'd had a stroke.

And which, at first, I decided to refute and refuse to believe – because I just had never thought of things the like of that ever happening to dogs – sustaining strokes the very same as humans.

But they do of course.

Me and the boys from Portrane – Peter, Tundish, Joe Squigs and Dr. Ken – we decided it only fair to have a proper funeral for him – he's buried there, underneath the linden at the bottom of the arboretum.

HERE LIES COLONEL BRUNO, MAN'S BEST FRIEND.

I wrote his epitaph myself, and you can see it on a little memorial that Peter the Painter carved especially.

Ken Milne did the honours of reading the service. And gave a little speech into the bargain. Everyone talked about how good it was, for weeks.

Not that Bruno was much of a dog. As a matter of fact, apart from being a loyal and extremely faithful companion, a role he fulfilled admirably, in so many other ways he simply wasn't worth a fuck.

Would you like to know what he did one day? Led me right through the back of Mrs. Beacon's private quarters, and her getting ready to have a fucking shower.

I mean – you can imagine.

Ee! Ee! – pulling a towel around her and all this.

I can't much remember what it used to be like before. In the days before that old 'Stevie.' Stevie Wonder, I mean. Before the blinds came down, ha ha!

I'm so glad you think it's funny, Martin Mooney – because I fucking don't.

That's what I often feel like saying to myself.

With the actual truth being there are days when I'd gladly give anything I own for just one second of the way it used to be.

When you could see all the birds poking their heads out from the linden, jerking away underneath the spreading green canopy, and Ken in his linen jacket walking around with his books, talking all this high-falutin' stuff.

And there by his side, as per usual, Dismal Tony. Who had been working for fifteen years on a book of poems – containing mostly verses about frogs and trees and, sometimes, wind.

His friend, presumably.

Ken would sometimes take us outside for our classes – right underneath the leaves of the linden, with the summer sun beaming down in the glorious open air. I can still hear Tony reading from his book, all shaky and nervous like he was going to get into trouble for reading it at all.

– I was sitting in my room this lovely fine February day, at a time when I was still very young and wondering just what on earth I might possibly do with my life. When, quite unexpectedly, all of a sudden I became aware of a mighty, crashing wind that had seemed to rise up completely out of nowhere, and in the process filled me with a great and vast unease and trepidatiousness. What could this possibly mean, I asked myself repeatedly, as I looked out the window and beheld the strangest of shapes and formations appearing in the sky. Whereupon I immediately went down to my parents in the kitchen and informed them of what I had just seen. When my father, who was sitting by the fire eating his dinner, looked over and said: if you don't give over that carry-on, Tony, I'll come over there and give you a box in the head. And that soon brought me to my senses.

I really have to say that I loved those times, and all those 'creative arts' classes with Dr. Ken Milne – and would do almost anything to have them back again.

Maybe just one second, one meagre scintilla. Of those now long-vanished, full-colour summer afternoons.

It breaks my heart, if you want to know the truth.

But I guess that's life – and like Fr. Ronnie says, we get what we deserve.

Although he wasn't talking about me, specifically.

We're living in Paradise and we don't even know it – that's the tragedy of being alive most – isn't it? Right down through all of the ages, he sometimes says.

– It's all there in front of us and we don't even see it.

Maybe the person reading this is exactly the very same – are you?

I couldn't say.

And it's hardly likely I'm ever going to know now – not after what's in store for me this weekend coming.

On the fifteenth day of April, exactly.

D-Day for Marty, I suppose you might call it.

But I'm looking forward to it – and have been all my life, I think, to be honest.

ALVY CARRAGHER

Alvy's first collection, *Falling in Love with Broken Things*, is available from Salmon Poetry. She was part of the 2016 Poetry Ireland Introduction Series, representing the series at a reading in New York. She graduated from the National University of Ireland Galway with a Masters in Writing, and returned to mentor/teach the third-year poetry workshop (2016 and 2017). She is currently living and teaching in South Korea.

An extract from *The Men I Keep Under My Bed*

up the carpeted stairs
trailing in leaves, dirt

it's not the kind of morning
for taking off my shoes

I'm sick of all that considering
tired of consequences

the full sweat of the run hits me
t-shirt limp from body heat

I nip into the bathroom
close the toilet, sit on its lid
elbows on knees, head in hands

what to do

in the mirror, drained, dark eyed
no pink in my cheeks

I rise, press my nose against my reflection
cold tap gushes, I cup my palm under the flow

scoop the waterfall over my face
dip my head, lips ducked under the tap
fill my mouth, swill it around
water warms, froths
I spit out the after-taste of sweaty spit

I can't go into the bedroom like this
I tug a brush through hair
pat concealer under eyes
smudge out the dark circles
a lashing of mascara

(no harm in looking closer to my best)

there's little I can do about the outfit,
suck my stomach in, resent my impulse to be thinner

he's asleep, doesn't hear me pad across the room
I stay quiet, find my most flattering clothes

it's not that I want him to fancy me
it's more like
I cannot let him see me

the last time I wore this dress
I felt good, it dipped
hugged the right places

but not today

today it's asking me not to force it

he coughs in his sleep
a tight knot climbs up my throat

I tip-toe towards the bed
retrieve my shoes from under it
black with a kitten heel

(I'll be crippled by 3pm)

(stop this, brain, whisht)

he rolls over in his sleep
I might escape without him waking

I reach for my fob and coat
place them on the back of the chair
before going to the kitchen

Sarah is sitting at the table
more dressing gown than human
face resting on her arms

she jumps when I enter

'so'

shouldn't you be in bed

'well yeah
but I wasn't going to wait all day for the news
so, did you'

did I what

I'm whispering

the idea of *him* hearing is too much
the idea of *him* waking is too much

'you know'

there's a smirk on her face
Sarah wants to be single

yeah

'and'

nothing special

'well the first time is never'

yeah

this will wait

I'll tell you later, I'm late

Alvy Carragher

I've work

'oh right, well I suppose
pre-coffee sex chats are not ideal'

there's a wink in her voice

yeah, I'll be good and
caffeinated by tonight

'will I get a bottle'

I'm about to say no, when out comes a yes
(isn't that always the fucking way with me)

in the bedroom, he has woken

gangly and naked
taking up more space than before
no longer curled into his sleep
pulling a t-shirt over his head
the dark brown curls of his chest disappear
the slight bump of his stomach gone

I stand in the door
he reaches down, checky boxers
the squares jig and blur

you're up

it is morning, can you go, what's your name, why did you
stay, do you've any manners you're not expecting breakfast,
are you, how does this keep happening to me

announces itself slowly in my head

but none of the words make it out

'I am, yeah'

all casual lean zipping up his jeans
giving me the once over
the sizing up, the decision
about whether he got lucky or not
if I'm worth boasting about

that's good

eyes stuck to my work fob
slung across the chair

I've work

I add
executing one of Mammy's sure what can you do
looks
the one she uses when she's no energy left to argue

'well I, eh, can I've your number'

he asks
but it's not a real question
the modern-day equivalent of etiquette
like asking a lady for a second dance
but bailing before the third

(back in the old days
or the eighties in the midlands
according to my mother)

from the way he asked
he will never use the number

unless drunk, unless 3am
unless desperate and lonely
unless Tinderless

I give it to him deadpan
let the sound fill up the room

'sound, I'll give you a text'

he tucks the phone into his back pocket

I gesture towards the door
I do not want him, but it hurts to be rejected
he got what he came for
maybe I'm bad at this

he gives me a cold kiss on the cheek
the kind offered up to dead people

forced out for grannies

he is gone

a minute later
Sarah is in the room

'jesus the state of the place
what were ye up to at all'

she indicates my clothes, scattered across the floor

'he was all right
if Diarmaid didn't have me nailed down
you'd be in for a bit of competition'

she moves to sit on the bed
I should be gone already

tonight, yeah

'pull a sickie, sure it's Friday
you'll do fuck all in there with the head on ya'

that would be the third this month
how would I explain

'the horrors of flu season'

she rolls fully onto the bed
stares at the wall

I'm out the door

'I'll be right here when you get back'

I force out a laugh

(a styrofoam stuffed with plastic sound)

I rush down the steps

I hear Sarah singing

to the ceiling in my room

CLAIRE HENNESSY

Claire Hennessy is the author of several YA novels, most recently *Nothing Tastes As Good* and *Like Other Girls*. She is a co-founder and co-editor of *Banshee* literary journal, and also works as a creative writing facilitator, editor, speaker and book reviewer.

The First Time

The first time you ever think about dying, really think about it, you're sitting in history class learning about the French Revolution. Ms Keating, your teacher, is trying to get everyone excited by giving them the gory details – even as Louisa beside you has her this-is-so-totally-gross face on, the same expression she regularly adopts in science class and when you dare offer an opinion on anything ever – and you listen to what it was like when they started guillotining people. There's a trashy *Sweet Valley* book you have somewhere, part of an older cousin's collection you inherited, that sets guillotines in forests in the middle of the night from the very beginning of the uprising, but this is apparently wrong (shocker, you think, but distantly, because you are frozen).

They don't start guillotining 'til later in the revolution, and then there is this whole thing about cheeks flushing when slapped, about being aware – like chickens, is it chickens that run around headless? – for a moment or two after your head has been removed. After that blade has sliced its way through your neck, and you are left looking at your body, those arms and legs that you have no control of anymore, that belly you always wished was smaller, those breasts you wished were bigger – and then. And then there is nothing.

And you know without a doubt that the nothing is coming for you and you can't stop it.

You're fourteen.

This is the first time.

It scares you the most, this time.

The first time you know death is when you are twelve, when in quick succession your grandmother, a school friend and a neighbour die. When the school friend dies you are still in the middle of your first period, a complicated matter involving sneaking pads out of your parents' bathroom (you cannot and will not tell your mother, how embarrassing, you are not living in a Judy Blume novel). It is during the summer and you are relieved to be able to wear black to the funeral, instead of bright florals that stain far too easily.

You should feel more than this, you know. You should be solemn and sad and distraught and crying like everyone else. Why can't you cry? Why is there something broken inside of you?

The first time you cut yourself you are fifteen and you have read about it in magazines and Problem Novels for teenagers, the kind that come with lists of helplines and resources at the back, except they are never relevant. Either they are American or

British, like Ireland doesn't exist, like no one in Ireland could possibly take the pink razor meant for their leg hair and drag it across their upper thighs so that pearls of blood rise to the surface.

You do not experience what the books call Dis-association, where you float out of your body and look at yourself like you are a stranger to it. You are still resolutely in this body, this container for your soul, if such a thing exists, and it has scabs forming.

Look at them. Look at them. They are beautiful. They are real.

Later, when you trace your fingertips over them, there is something almost erotic about the sting of pain.

The first time you tell your dad that maybe you should see a counsellor, he raises his eyebrows in that way you know means 'notions'. Patiently, though: 'Angie, why do you think you need a counsellor?'

'I just —' All the words vanish from your brain.

It is not that your dad doesn't approve of counselling. He would be a fool and hypocrite not to. But counselling is for people with real problems. Kids whose parents beat them or neglect them. That girl down the road whose eating disorder is so bad that she runs away every fortnight, and has been found more than once going through the bins outside the nearest McDonald's. That boy he referred to counselling with burns up and down his arms (burns are worse than cuts; you don't know how you know this but you do).

Other people have real problems and you – you —

You are sixteen years old and nothing bad, really, has ever happened to you. You have a roof over your head. You have a father who tells you to follow your heart when it comes to picking your Leaving Cert subjects and a mother who agonizes over you making the wrong choices and they both mean so well that it hurts your heart.

You feel it there, at night, your heart. It is too heavy somehow. And you cannot blame your parents or the media or video games or Facebook or whatever people are blaming for teenage angst these days.

It just hurts, that's all. And the problem is not the world. It's you.

The first time you tell your mother you're sick is when you are seven years old.

She tells you to get out of bed anyway. You don't have a temperature. And you know you don't have a temperature, but you feel you should have. You must. Because there is something else happening, something else that your body is telling you: you need to be in bed. You *need* to not go to school.

She sends you to school. You don't have a temperature. And you don't collapse or anything dramatic like that. The volume is turned down on your life, is all.

But you don't have a temperature. So you're not really sick. So you can still go to school.

You only stay off school unless you're really, properly sick, you see.

The first time you get drunk you're eighteen and you love it. This is the missing puzzle piece. You kiss boys you never thought you could ever dare approach. You dance with girls from school that you thought you hated; you even make out with Louisa at one point, in someone's back garden, while painfully-retro 80s music blares out from the kitchen. This is legal and this is practically encouraged. You go to your cousin's wedding, the one whose books you still have in your bedroom, and she is delighted to buy you wine, and cocktails, and shots.

And so what if you feel like death in the morning, so fucking what.

At least there is a reason for it.

The first time you show a boy your scars you're seventeen and he runs his tongue along them in worship.

He has them too, up and down his arms. But he says this thing you don't quite understand: 'obviously you're much worse than me,' is what he says.

It's not an insult. It is, in its own weird way, a compliment to fucked-up-ness, an admission of guilt, a recognition of something serious going on.

Except that it feels like when someone tells you that you look gorgeous and immediately your instinct is to deflect: *oh no I borrowed this. Oh wouldja stop. Ah sure – Penney's finest!*

The first time you fuck up an exam is when you're twenty, which is actually pretty good going, seeing as how you spent significant chunks of your first year of college in the bar arguing with classmates about books and theories and politics and which cheap alcohol was the best value.

You have to have a meeting with the head of department, and among his suggestions is this: counselling.

So you go and wait, oddly excited by the whole thing, and then you see Evie, star of half your tutorials last year, and you know suddenly that you cannot compete with whatever troubles Evie might have.

Your parents reluctantly agree to pay for you to repeat the year, yet with slight relief that you have not been deemed crazy enough to repeat free of charge For Medical Reasons, and the guilt is enough to ensure that you spend the first two weeks of lectures with a duvet over your head. You tell your parents that classes start back weirdly late this year.

The first time a counsellor suggests antidepressants, you're twenty-two and in love with an older guy, not that much older but old enough, and he has really strong feelings about this – they turn you into a zombie, fry your brain, make you feel not-quite-real. And you've finals coming up and you don't want to screw them up the way you have with exams before, so you say no.

All throughout finals you wear a heavy cardigan to cover up the razor-blade scratches on your arms, even though summer has kicked off early and it's really too hot in the exam halls to wear wool. You're a grown-up now. You don't want to look as though you're seeking attention.

You tell your boyfriend it's the family cat, expecting him not to believe you. To look into your eyes and ask: what's wrong? What can I do to help? Have you thought about...

He nods and continues undressing you.

The first time you call in sick to work you are twenty-four and it's a hangover, because a hangover comes with proper symptoms: throwing up and headaches and a general weariness that is somehow better and more worthy than everyday weariness.

It's a joy, it is, calling in sick. When you do it you can't remember the last time you did this and then you think: never. You were never allowed miss a day of secondary school in your life, and college never demanded phoned-in explanations for absenteeism. To miss a lecture or two, a tutorial or three – normal.

It's gorgeous, this. To have the day to yourself and to breathe easy, knowing that you are off the hook for work. For life. For everything.

The first time the doctor talks about antidepressants, like you don't know what they are, you tell him no. He seems relieved and then tells you about exercise. Exercise and fruit.

Your mother is losing her own mother in a haze of dementia and kidney stuff you block out the intricate details of. Your father has just retired and is coping badly with empty days and hopeful phone calls to former colleagues gone unanswered. You are twenty-six and a brat, a privileged monster who has no right to feel bad.

You don't do the exercise.

You don't eat the fruit.

It is not that you don't believe they work. You know they do, for some people.

The thought of it just makes you want to kill yourself.

The first time you think about it properly:

Look. You love the Luas. The purple and yellow, like a bruise, zooming towards you. You remember vaguely: your cynical childhood, insistent that they would never finish it, 'akhtually'. You charmed neighbours and relatives, but at the end of the day you were wrong. Foolish. Stupid.

Every time the Luas hurtles towards your stop, you imagine stepping out in front of it. It would be so easy.

You have everything to live for except that your body hasn't quite figured this out yet. And twice a day, at least – into work, out of work – you steel your faithless body against the treacherous urge to fling yourself into harm's way.

You're twenty-eight and you're not supposed to feel like this anymore except you do.

All.

the.

time.

The first time you call a helpline you have consumed, oh, let's say a bottle of wine.

Or two.

Or three.

You want them to say: we will send someone out to you right now.

You want them to say: you need to be in hospital. Being minded.

You want them to say anything but: hang on in there.

Fuck. That. Shit.

You are too worn-out to save yourself.

Eat more fruit.

Go for a nice brisk walk.

Meet a friend for tea (herbal, ideally).

Funny how when you squint it all looks like: pull your fucking socks up.

It's not that you want to die.

It is just that this is so exhausting, all of it. It is like you have signed a contract to let people down.

Your family are disappointed you are not spending enough time with them.

Your friends judge you for not making that dinner. Those drinks.

Your boss disapproves of you slipping out early of Christmas drinks.

Here are the things you want to do:

1. Sleep
2. Sleep
3. Eat
4. Drink
5. Sleep

You don't want to be here, wherever here is. Dublin. Ireland. Earth. Awake.

You sleep with a guy from work because Carrie who you went to school with thinks you need to get laid, and basically you just cry all over him once he comes (you don't, of course you don't, and you can't expect any guy to bother making that happen) and it is deeply humiliating.

And that should be the end of it except that you sleep with another guy from work. This one you tell: 'I'm depressed.'

He finds this fascinating, which is infinitely creepier than being put off by it, and he is disappointed when you reveal that you are not medicated. He looks at you like you have told him the worst lie in the world. He doesn't talk to you ever again.

You take the medication.

Already this first time and the other times, the future times, are blurring into one.

It will not work instantly.

It takes time.

And yet that first week sees you skipping up streets and wide-eyed all the way. The sun. The sky. The flowers. The world is beautiful. It is all so, so beautiful.

It does not cure everything but look: the world is so, so beautiful.

Some things you do on this miracle medication, after the first three months: drink too much. Cut yourself. Sleep with inappropriate men. Feel. Like. Shit.

You try another one.

You sit with a glass of half-drunk wine and a kitchen knife and jesus it is too much effort to cut yourself so you might as well just – sleep.

This is not a cure.

This is not not-a-cure.

You are smart and clever and you are supposed to be fixed with something more sophisticated than a daily tablet. You are more nuanced. More complex.

You flush all your pills.

The boy – man – who wants to sleep with you does not like that you burst into tears when he is nice to you.

You breathe in and out and look at the number on your phone. The doctor that can prescribe you the antidepressants that will fix – in due course, blah blah blah – you.

You are thirty years old and you are so, so tired of being tired.

You think of Dorothy Parker and you feel clever and sassy for doing so. Quite frankly. Look how literary you are, thinking of Parker's poem about suicide when you're pondering methods yourself. It is so apt. So – so – so something.

You don't want to die.

You don't want to live.

You leave the roof of the building and you go home to your parents' house and despair over the obvious things like the economy and not the voices in your head that whisper and whimper and coerce and tell you: *you're better off dead.*

Objectively, the economy is –

– *You're better off dead* –

– terrible, and we must remember –

– *Some people are just worthless...*

And aren't you? Objectively? Objectively, how the fuck are you not fucking worthless? You at thirty-one, you with an arts degree and a handful of work experience bits 'n' pieces that accumulates to nothing, really, nothing at all. You're shit. It's not hyperbole, it's true. You. Are. Shit. You have nothing to offer.

Why

don't

you

just

die

because you are the worst of everything they talk about in the papers, entitled millennials, snowflakes, the kind of people who thought they should be able to get a job (but was that so wrong?) after their degree and the kind of people that wonder now why on earth they can't make any money, because they didn't – didn't work hard enough? Or just didn't get born at the right time?

…fuck, it's endless.

So you breathe in and you tell your parents that you are delighted to be there.

That you will stay for as long as they'll let you.

That you don't know when you'll be ready to leave

(because who is?)

The first time you are ready, really ready, it's an ordinary day. You're thirty-three and you're still living with your parents and like it has always been there, it slots into place: you're always going to be sick.

And maybe the 'sick' should feel like a burden and maybe the 'always' should feel like a death sentence but the truth is you realise you are once again afraid of dying.

It is your Catholic upbringing, you think. Thirty-three: Jesus when he was crucified.

Crucifixion – suffocation, really – seems even worse than the guillotine. At least the latter is quick.

But you don't want either. Not today. (You're always going to be sick, though.)

You ring the doctor.

Counsellor tomorrow (baby steps).

It would be ideal if the sun was shining, but this is Ireland and autumn and it is raining, lashing down, and you watch the drops pelt the kitchen window with something that is not quite a smile, but not quite not, either.

LILLIAN ALFORD PATTERSON

Lillian Alford Patterson is a writer from Mississippi, currently living between Dublin and New Orleans, Louisiana. She holds a Bachelors of Literature and Creative Writing from Bard College, and a Masters of Philosophy in Creative Writing from Trinity College. Lillian volunteers with Fighting Words while in Dublin and for Big Class while in New Orleans. While her literary focus has been in nonfiction, she is currently working on a novel about the people of New Orleans post-Katrina. This is her first piece published in Ireland.

An excerpt from *All of the Houses I Have Lived In*

Three months after his death the tail end of my car was pulled up to Melissa's house. The porch was littered with boxes, poorly packed; books and photographs overflowed from them. I insisted on taking them all, in part as an anchor to ground myself with, in part because I feared my stepmother would throw them away or donate them to charity.

It was midmorning, late August in Mississippi, hot and oppressive. Sweat poured down my neck, my back, and into my shorts. The moisture created a distinct line, the shape of my spine. My stepmother reminded me to shut the door every time we brought a new box out. Frugal to the point of annoyance. Each time I carried out a box, I looked back to the house. The house that was never my home. Only on the holidays and the odd summer.

I loaded the boxes. I positioned them carefully, then wove in my malleable belongings like pillows and blankets, making one solid block. There was no space remaining. I tried to force in a few last things; a small shelf decorated with teal blown glass bobbles that belonged to my namesake, a crocheted portrait of birds nesting in a tree, a family heirloom but from whom I could not remember. I asked my sister to keep them for me. I did not say until when. In the moment I did not want to indicate when I would be coming back for good because the truth was, I did not know.

My father's ashes were the last item I packed. My stepmother asked me if I would like to take the urn. I said no. I thought that my father would not have liked the thing, it being too ornate. My sister kept his ashes in a Hill Brothers' coffee can. It was purchased after my father pronounced 'I don't care what you do to me, put me in a goddamn Hill Brothers' coffee can.' I took what I had of him – approximately one third – in a plastic Ziploc bag with the intention of transferring the ashes into a more appropriate receptacle later. I never did.

I needed to put distance between that house, him, my own grief, the version of myself that I would leave there and what I hoped to become.

As I drove out of town all I could smell was Molly. She was my father's dog. Her foul breath filled the car. I turned off the air conditioning, trying to keep its circulation contained. I rolled down the window and hoped she would stick her head out. She looked up at me, unaware. Molly had come into our home at the time when my mother left. It had been my father, Molly and me for so long. She was the emblem of the relationship I had built with my father over those years in which we had both been abandoned. She had provided us both with comfort. I craved that comfort in his absence. I insisted on taking her. She had been ours.

On that first day, I drove for miles into a western setting sun. I thought that my eyes had never faced into a descending sun for such a long time. They burned. I had to blink to keep my vision clear. The sun fell in the west and blazed through the windows of the car, the vehicle so packed I could not use my rear mirror. I couldn't look back or perhaps I truly did not want to. I was twenty-three years old. I felt like a child. My father was gone and my home had gone with him.

I crossed the border into South Eastern Montana. As I drove into Billings, I saw refineries erect and defined against deep black sky. They did not light up the dark sky but instead hid the stars with the pollution that they exuded. High above me were towers that burned with yellow bulbs, a city within a city. Some were steady, some blinked intermittently. Tiny puffs of smoke hovered in the distance. The smoke stacks must have been painted dark, as the small clouds seemed to appear from nothing and just as quickly disappeared. Stadium lights projected down into the centre of the industrial landscape, no doubt to provide the night labourers with light. I checked in at a Red Roof Inn, because it was cheap and allowed pets. Slightly unclean and filled with the smell of bleach.

The air was thick with chemicals and the sheets on the mattress scratched at my skin. I held Molly close to me; her acrid breath covered the stench of bleach.

My sleep was restless. An embodiment of agitation entered my dreams. Huge, it loomed above me. It whispered cynicism and fear. It was dark and strange and the more I ran from it, the faster it came. I woke early in the morning. I loaded the car and bought a cup of black acidic gas station coffee. I drank it quickly and paid for another.

As I drove from the city, I saw the Rimrocks. Sandstone formations that rose from the earth at a gradual incline then jutted vertically and plateaued. A portrait of the rise and fall of waterways, they were alien, cut from a river that came long before any of our memories.

The altitude rose as I headed farther west into Montana. The plains of the east quickly fell behind the height of the mountains. Native American tribes once retreated into this range in the winter, using them as protection from the biting winds.

I crossed the Missouri River, its origin in the Rocky Mountains, swelling and contracting with the changing of the seasons and the melting of winter. It was broad and deep and blue. Its bed was composed of stones. The shapes of the stones contorted and wavered as the pellucid water flowed over them. It travels two thousand, three hundred and thirty-four miles to empty into the Mississippi. The sun danced on the surface. I thought 'If I got on a boat here and just let it flow, it would take me back.'

I took the North side exit to enter Missoula. I passed through a tunnel decorated with local graffiti, a foreign language to my eyes. I crossed the Higgins

Street Bridge and looked down into the basin of the river. The rocks were exposed grey and cracking, so much more beautiful when covered by the running water. I had travelled two thousand, one hundred, and eighty-five miles.

My first house in Missoula was on South Third Street NW. I moved in during early September. Molly wove around and through my legs as I unloaded boxes from the car and carried them through the front door. She buried her nose in every corner and took in all this unfamiliar space that would now be her home.

I had not brought furniture with me; the car was only packed with what was essential or what I deemed to be so. My books, clothes, and my photographs. I carried my history, but I kept it to myself, hidden in my room, just for me. I knew that I had to try to start over, but I wanted the option to go back.

I bought a ratty couch from a second-hand store owned by the church. I sprayed it with disinfectant and vacuumed it over and over. I eventually covered it with a sheet. I bought a second-hand mattress and placed it on the hardwood floor. Molly would share this bed with me. I used a milk crate as a nightstand and faced the opening outward to serve as a small bookshelf. I placed my books in stacks around the room. Precarious towers. Makeshift surfaces.

The room was painted tangerine. I despised the colour but never asked to change it. To change anything would have felt too permanent. I did not want to become a fixture. The floors were exposed wood. I was not sure what kind. They were scratched and marked. Furniture had been dragged in and out of this home. I wondered if the former tenants also saw it as some sort of halfway house.

I tacked my father's obituary to the wall. I had written it in May at the time of his death. Along with it I hung a poem my parents received as a wedding present, framed, the paper yellowed. It was an unintentional shrine. I placed my father's ashes behind the books in the milk crate. I didn't touch them again until the following spring, the anniversary of his death.

By the summer of 2013 my alcoholism was huge but functional. I had taken a job at a small bakery. It allowed me to keep early hours so my evenings could be given to drinking. I found that I wasn't able to sleep without the help of a bottle of wine.

One evening I sat up late at one of the local bars. I struck up a conversation with the man next to me. Drunk enough to forget his face, I do not recall our conversation at all. He reminded me later that he was just coming through town, a traveller on his way south from Alaska. I allowed him into my house. He smelled like smouldering wood and sweat. I closed my eyes as the layer of fat on his stomach moved against my abdomen. When he was done I rolled over and fell into sleep. He was gone when I woke the following morning and I was glad. No trace left except for the smell on my sheets, which I washed immediately.

Two weeks later I drove into the mountains with a man I had met when I first arrived in Missoula. He had shown no interest in me until that evening. Up we drove to look out over the city. I held a beer in my hand and he held one between his knees and took long swigs then cracked the seal of another. The uneven road jostled us and I began to feel sick but said nothing. Finally we stopped, we sat on the hood of the car and looked up at the stars. He kissed me, first sweetly then vigorously. He jumped down from the hood and pulled me by the hand. He turned me around, leaned me against the truck, pulled up my skirt, and pushed himself into me. It was quick and silent. When he finished he sat back on the hood of the truck, drank two more beers, then drove me home. After he pulled away I vomited in my front yard. Whether it was from the alcohol or the jostling of the car, or my own disgust with myself I am not sure.

I could not admit my own unhappiness. I was an expert in denial, too scared to ask for help, and too proud to admit that there was something awful happening within me. I was lonelier than I had ever felt and I was allowing myself to drown in it. I became good at hiding these flaws. I found that if I insisted to myself each morning that I was happy, even simply that I was okay, then everyone around me would believe it too. They had not known me before, so why would they expect different. I fabricated aspects of my past. White lies I told myself.

I told stories, ones about my father. I uttered them – trying to mimic his way, the gesticulations and eagerness – then immediately wondered if they were true. I wondered if these stories were the truth of my father or memories that I had invented. I told these stories out of fear. I told these stories to live them again. If they were not repeated they would be forgotten so I searched for opportunities to retell them. I noticed that with each telling a piece disappeared but I was never certain which bit had vanished. I told the stories to try to pull them back to myself and hold tight to them because the truth was that I was beginning to forget.

My one friend, William, lived across the bridge. I often cycled over late at night once I had grown tired of drinking alone. He gave me beer and cooked steaks that he would burn black with butter on the outside and leave bloody in the middle. After we ate, we sat in the back yard. We smoked cigarettes and talked until I would reach my cusp, unable to drink anymore if I wished to return home.

On this evening I listened to the sound of the Clark Fork River as I pedalled toward his home. The river moved rapidly next to me, the water swelled and took over the bank. Snow runoff from the tops of Bitterroot Range. It was still summer although the heat had begun to fade and autumn would settle soon. The evening had cooled but my hair was matted from the day's sweat. I was a little drunk. I could smell the beer on my breath as I exhaled heavily; my lungs were tight from the pace. I wore a sundress. It was not fitted and flapped behind me, no doubt exposing the tops of my thighs. I wore boots. They were loose around my ankles. My socks were moist with sweat.

I reached the pedestrian bridge to cross from the south to the north side of the city. Its span went four hundred feet across the water and was hung by cables and a single iron tower. The planks of wood groaned as they expanded and contracted with the changing seasons. It was well lit in the evenings, each end illuminated by street lamps.

On most evenings I weaved through the bollards and crossed the bridge giving little attention to anything but my destination. This evening a fading light caught me. I stopped to watch it. Over and over it flickered at me. A short circuit. A disconnect. Flashed then fizzled. It blinked rapidly twelve times then on the thirteenth; the light sustained and irradiated the bright green foliage of the tree behind it. It continued this way, and as I stood straddling my bicycle, the summer night hummed and spoke.

I began to cry. It was the first time I had cried since his funeral. I did not move from the path. Twice every minute I was brought back into the light with the violent flash of the dying bulb. The tears and my sweat mixed. I could not differentiate them, both hot and salty. I waited for a moment then mounted the bike seat and continued to William's house. Before I knocked on his door, I made sure my cheeks were not streaked. As I stood in his kitchen I told him about the light. I used the word 'Ethereal'. I tried to make sense not of what I had seen, but rather the word and why it had come to me. I repeated the word as I described it. I did not tell him about my tears.

The following May I took my father's ashes to the mountains for a second time. It was exactly two years since his death. On this occasion, the snow had melted and the path was so muddy that I moved along with delicate steps as though I were drunk. On my back I carried a bag that held the ashes and the last letter he wrote me. I carried them together as tradition.

I was alone in a forest of thick conifers. I followed the path and the sound of running water. I searched for the sound of water colliding with stone, surging in frothy white. I admired the spring wildflowers as I walked, the softness of their petals and their brilliant colours. I tried to name them like my father taught me but the names evaded me. I plucked one and rubbed the petals between my fingers. The smell was familiar but I could not place it. I dropped the blossom in the mud and continued on.

I listened for movement but there was nothing, just the fidgets of songbirds in the trees and the squelches beneath my feet. I knew I should not be in the forest alone. I had been told there were bears but this day was for my father and me only. There could not be space for others.

I could feel the air become colder; there was a fine mist that settled on my skin as I passed through it. The damp air meant that I was getting close.

I could hear the tumble down of water. It was the sound of many voices, all wanting to be heard. Ahead of me, I saw the falls. The water broke over the edge and cascaded down, down many feet before it settled into a slow and wide stream. I sat next to the stream and felt the sun. The stones around me were many shades of blues and purples and reds. I skipped them on the still surface, listened to them skim then sink into the water, watched the undulations as they grew rapidly, expansively, until they disappeared.

I walked up the stream to the base of the falls. I looked up, then placed my right foot carefully before I began to climb. The boulders were slick and mossy. I was careful with my step, moving on the balls of my feet like my father taught me. I stayed low as I climbed up and up until I reached the top. There I stood straight and looked out from the height. From this vantage I could see the Swans, still capped with snow. I thought it was a romantic name for a mountain range.

I reached in to the bag and pulled out the letter. I read it slowly and in a whisper. I said the words aloud for myself, 'I close this letter without writing to you about the future or the past. Those things are very much in front of you and very much behind you at this time. What I will tell you is that you should look to the future without worrying about seeing anything. Whatever you think it is, is probably something else. You are filled with a love of life that is brave and loud and alive with a furious desire to touch the things you sense are beyond the frontier of the moment. You are a remarkable child. I know – I know, but I am your father and you will always be my daughter and my child.' I was pulled back to the mornings that my father waited for me to wake. I was pulled back to the nights that I spent in the hospital, a chair next to his bed, my hand slid beneath his. From the bag I pulled the ashes. I took just a small amount in the palm of my hand. I released my father into the breeze and watched the silver grey dust rain down on the water. It carried my father down, down, and away from me. That night I did not dream.

ACKNOWLEDGEMENTS

This anthology could not have been without the generous help of so many. I am grateful to Mairead and Colette at the Dublin Rape Crisis Centre, who first heard the idea and supported it from the start; and to Noeline, who offered such warmth, belief and positivity. Huge thanks to Kerrie O'Brien for laying the magnificent groundwork for a project such as this with *Looking at the Stars*, and for being so giving of much-needed advice, help and direction. I am thankful also to Dan and Mariel at New Island Books who supported the project in various ways from the beginning, not to mention providing the collection with a large number of its wonderful writers. Thank you, Mariel, for all your help with the typesetting. Huge thanks also go to the Irish Writers Centre, who supported the project on many levels – including providing it with its launch space. Enormous thanks are due to Paul and Mark at Mutiny Publishing, who supported the anthology at a crucial time, and who are always supportive and lovely in general. I am thankful to Mark Weir (www.markweir.me), who built us a slick website, **thebrokenspiralbook.com**, and to everyone who continues to support the project via this website and on social media. Huge thanks also go to Sarah Quinn and Naomi McArdle, who tirelessly and inventively helped with all the behind the scenes activity and secured the sponsorship necessary to take the collection from idea into reality. Thank you Aoife McArdle for your help, also. Thank you to Cathy Brady for being the crucial link for so many things, and a great support during the process. I am grateful to Aoife and Niamh at Pink Kong, who created gorgeous cover art for the anthology, and to Ruza Leko of studiosuss.ie who designed the wonderful launch invites. I am also enormously thankful to Joanna Smyth and Alex Reece Abbott for offering their much-needed proofreading skills; and to Jean, Natasha and Kwamie Liv for being my first readers. Huge thanks also to Dubray, Books Upstairs and Hodges Figgis for stocking the book. Enormous thanks are due to our sponsors, Dublin UNESCO City of Literature, Bodytonic, Jane Chadwick and Mutiny Publishing, whose support made *The Broken Spiral* possible. Finally, I am grateful to every wonderful author who supported the project with their work; without them this book could not have been.